P9-CDA-599

333.72
C594c2

Phillips Library
Bethany College
Bethany, W. Va. 26032

DISCARD

DISCARD

CAREERS IN CONSERVATION

CAREERS IN CONSERVATION

Opportunities in Natural Resource Management

SECOND EDITION

Edited for the
Natural Resources Council
of America
by

HENRY CLEPPER

Natural Resources Council of America

A Ronald Press
Publication

JOHN WILEY & SONS

New York / Chichester
Brisbane / Toronto

Copyright © 1963, 1979 by John Wiley & Sons, Inc.

All rights reserved. Published simultaneously in Canada.

Reproduction or translation of any part of this work
beyond that permitted by Sections 107 or 108 of the
1976 United States Copyright Act without the permission
of the copyright owner is unlawful. Requests for
permission or further information should be addressed to
the Permissions Department, John Wiley & Sons, Inc.

Library of Congress Cataloging in Publication Data:

Clepper, Henry Edward, 1901-   ed.
  Careers in conservation.

  "A Ronald Press publication."
  Includes index.
  1.   Conservation of natural resources—Vocational
guidance. I.   Natural Resources Council of America.
II.   Title.

S945.C55   1979   333.7'2'023   78-21917
ISBN 0-471-05163-2

Printed in the United States of America

10 9 8 7 6 5 4 3 2 1

The Contributors

HUGH O. CANHAM
is Associate Professor in the Department of Managerial Science and Policy of the State University of New York College of Environmental Science and Forestry at Syracuse. He has taught courses and completed research projects in resource economics and land-use planning.

HENRY CLEPPER
holds the chair of the Publications Committee of the Natural Resources Council of America. For twenty-eight years he was Managing Editor of the *Journal of Forestry* and Executive Secretary of the Society of American Foresters. He is author or editor of ten books on natural resource conservation.

KENNETH P. DAVIS
is Professor Emeritus of Land Use of the Yale University School of Forestry and Environmental Studies. He is author of *Forest Management: Regulation and Evaluation*, and *Land Use*, and is coauthor of *Forest Fire: Control and Use*. He is a past President of the Society of American Foresters.

DAVID R. DeWALLE
is Associate Professor of Forest Hydrology in the School of Forest Resources of The Pennsylvania State University at University Park. He teaches courses in Watershed Management and Forest Microclimatology, and is currently a member of the Steering Committee of the Association of University Watershed Scientists.

333.72
C594c2

FRED G. EVENDEN

has been Executive Director of The Wildlife Society in Washington, D.C., since 1963. Formerly he was a Wildlife Research Biologist for the U.S. Fish and Wildlife Service and Executive Director of the California Junior Museum. He has been an officer and committeeman in many national organizations benefiting natural resources conservation.

ROBERT M. HYDE

Extension Range Scientist at Colorado State University, has numerous publications on range management and improvement. He has been an extension range scientist in Wyoming and Kansas, and has B.S. and M.S. degrees from Fort Hays Kansas State University and a Ph.D. in range science from the University of Wyoming.

ORLO M. JACKSON

now retired, was Acting Director of Professional Programs for the Society of American Foresters, Washington, D.C. He was formerly Director of Personnel Management for the U.S. Forest Service, Washington, D. C.

WALTER E. JESKE

is Chief of the Education and Publications branch of the Soil Conservation Service, U.S. Department of Agriculture, Washington, D.C. He holds the chair of the Subcommittee on Environmental Education of the Federal Interagency Committee on Education and has served as National Vice President of the Soil Conservation Society of America.

ROBERT T. LACKEY

is Associate Professor and Section Leader of Fisheries Science at Virginia Polytechnic Institute and State University at Blacksburg. He holds the chair of the Professional Education Standards Committee of the American Fisheries Society, and has published several books and many articles on fisheries and wildlife management.

ARTHUR B. MEYER

has served as Assistant State Forester of Missouri, is a former Editor of the *Journal of Forestry*, and is now Technical Editor of the Division of the Environment, Bureau of Mines, U.S. Department of the Interior, Washington, D.C.

ERIC D. PRINCE

is a Fishery Research Biologist with the U.S. Fish and Wildlife Service in South Carolina. He is a Certified Fisheries Scientist of the American Fisheries Society and a member of the American Institute of Fishery Research Biologists. He has written scientific and popular articles on marine, estuarine, and freshwater fisheries management.

GRANT W. SHARPE

is Professor of Outdoor Recreation in the College of Forest Resources of the University of Washington at Seattle. He received his Ph.D. degree in Forest Ecology and Recreation. He is a coauthor of *Introduction to American Forestry* and editor and coauthor of *Interpreting the Environment*, and is a cofounder of the Association of Interpretive Naturalists.

WILLIAM E. SOPPER

is Professor of Forest Hydrology in the School of Forest Resources of The Pennsylvania State University at University Park. He is Associate Editor for the *Journal of Forestry*, *Journal of Water Resources Research*, and *Journal of Environmental Quality*, and is a coeditor of a book on *Forest Hydrology*.

VERLON K. VRANA

is Assistant Administrator for Management of the Soil Conservation Service, U.S. Department of Agriculture, Washington, D.C. He received a Superior Service Award from USDA in 1977.

Dedicated to
Samuel Trask Dana

1883-1978

Sometime Dean of the
University of Michigan
School of Natural Resources
and
Doyen of Conservation Education
in America

Preface

A career in conservation—that is, working with natural resources—can be, and is for thousands of men and women, a satisfying and rewarding lifetime employment. With the rise of the environmental movement during the 1960s, the urgent need for the wise use of all natural resources became a national issue, and many young people were encouraged to join this worthy cause and to prepare for careers by obtaining professional and scientific educations.

As a result, college enrollments in the traditional conservation curriculums—for example, fisheries, forestry, marine biology, range management, park and outdoor recreation, and wildlife management—have been rising. Students enrolled in such curriculums are usually well informed about the technical work for which they are preparing.

But many other young people know little about the duties of the professional in natural resources. Often their interest springs from an emotional concept—they want to stop oil spills, or protect endangered animals, or prevent clearcutting of timber. In short, they seek involvement in the environmental movement without getting the educational preparation necessary to make them employable. There is no adequate substitute for a professional or scientific education for one seeking a professional or scientific career.

Conservation is on the march. It has become more and more attractive to young people. There are good jobs, interesting work, and rewards over and above compensation (although salaries have been on the rise).

That conservation is a relatively young profession gives a certain advantage to those entering it, because much remains to be learned about the wise use of natural resources, the protection of the environment, and the renewal of environmental quality. Hence there are many opportunities for research and new ideas, for the development of new techniques, and for solving the many challenging soil and water problems. Conservation needs ambitious young workers. It offers healthful work usually in the outdoors, adequate compensation, and the personal satisfaction one feels in helping make a stronger nation and a better land in which to live. There are now more people employed in natural resources than at any time in the past fifty years.

This book was prepared to answer many of the thousands of inquiries received each year—by state and federal conservation agencies, by conservation associations and professional societies, and by educational institutions—from young men and women seeking information about careers in natural resources. In this book are described eleven fields of specialization traditionally considered the basis of conservation, with separate chapters written by specialists who, each in his own profession, are well qualified to advise on the educational preparation needed for careers in that field.

Careers in Conservation was first published in 1963. The present edition has been updated and completely revised. The authors hope that the book will be helpful, not alone to students, but also to their parents and educational counselors. It is sponsored by the Natural Resources Council of America, a nonprofit, nonpolitical organization of forty-six national and regional associations and societies dedicated to the conservation and wise use of our natural resources and the environment. I am grateful to the authors for their cooperation.

HENRY CLEPPER

Washington, D.C.
November 1978

Contents

1 Education for Careers in Resource Management

HENRY CLEPPER

Young men and women who are planning for the future, charting their own life work or helping others whom they may be called upon to advise, may wish to consider careers in conservation. There are opportunities for capable, responsible, properly trained people in work concerned with our natural resources. It is useful work. It can be pleasant and rewarding. To point out some of the major fields in which these opportunities lie and to indicate what kind of preparation and education may be needed are the purposes of this book.

Conservation of natural resources—what does it mean? In its old-time dictionary sense, the word "conservation" meant to protect or preserve something from loss, decay or injury. When it is applied to natural resources, conservation has a broader meaning. It has to do not only with husbanding resources through wise use but with perpetuating or replenishing them by development and management.

Some natural resources exist in fixed amounts. We can increase our supplies of iron or petroleum by discovering new deposits or by developing better methods of extraction. Vast amounts undoubtedly remain to be exploited. But the total amounts of these materials contained in the earth cannot be increased. Iron, coal, sulfur, and other minerals therefore are known as nonrenewable resources. The conservation of such resources is a matter of avoiding waste, of using them efficiently and wisely.

THE RENEWABLE RESOURCES

Certain other natural resources are renewable. Trees and grasses, fish, and wildlife can renew themselves naturally. Or they can be made to reproduce themselves and yield continuing "crops" under scientific management. Of necessity, those concerned with such resources must be interested also in the soil and water that support them. Thus soil and water, too, in a sense, are renewable resources. Soil can be improved through skillful management and made more usable. We cannot control the amount of rain that falls on the earth—not yet—but with knowledge and skill we can improve the quality and perpetuate the supplies of water available for our use.

This book is concerned with renewable natural resources. The career opportunities described have to do with the scientific management of forests and rangelands, water and soil, fish and wildlife. Included also are the related fields of work in general biology, land use, and outdoor recreation.

Renewable natural resources are essential to human welfare. Our lives depend on the availability of usable water and productive soil. Wood is one of the basic raw materials of our industries.

Our forests help to provide material for our homes and for hundreds of the commodities we use in our everyday living. Wood is used in many of our tools and implements and in the processing of most other materials. From wood come paper products, certain textiles, and a number of plastics and chemicals. Research and advancing technology are constantly expanding its uses and adding to the number of products made from wood.

Our natural grassland ranges contribute to our food supply by furnishing forage for millions of livestock. They are the home, too, of important species of wildlife.

Trees and shrubs of the forests and grass on the ranges are essen-

Gifford Pinchot, America's first native professional forester and the foremost conservationist of his era. (Photo by U.S. Forest Service.)

tial in maintaining our water supplies. They help to hold the soil in place, control the runoff of water from rain or melting snow, and regulate the flow of streams. Without the protection of forests and grasses on our mountains and hills, water would rush down in destructive torrents after every heavy storm. It would wash soil and gravel from the hills into the valleys and down the stream courses into our bays and harbors. Between rains the streams would dry up. Our country would be a barren, unproductive waste—as indeed parts of it now are.

Forests and ranges contribute to our health and pleasure by providing opportunities for outdoor recreation. Millions of people enjoy sightseeing, hiking, riding, picnicking, and camping in the forests, fishing in the oceans, streams, and lakes, and hunting in the woods or on the range. Skiing attracts thousands to winter-sports areas in the forests and parks. Fish and wildlife and outdoor recreation activities have economic as well as enjoyment values. The businesses and manufacturing enterprises serving sports lovers and vacationers bring employment and income to thousands and play a significant part in the national economy. Birds and other insect eaters are of tremendous value in helping to control the pests that plague our agriculture. Fresh and saltwater fishing provides an important part of our food supply.

Less tangible, but nevertheless real, are the social, aesthetic, and spiritual values of the outdoors. Scenic beauty is one of the things that make us proud of our country. To preserve some of our outstanding scenic attractions, we have wisely put extensive areas into national and state parks. Many areas of unspoiled wilderness have been set aside within our national forests, parks, and other public lands. Contact with nature enriches our lives. Green fields and forests, clear, cool waters contribute, perhaps more than we realize, to mental health and to relief from today's problems and pressures.

THE RISE OF CONSERVATION

America has been blessed with an abundance of natural resources. Through lavish use of these resources, our nation has been able to build its great industries, constantly improve its standard of living and achieve a leading position among the nations of the world. If our country is to progress, we must continue to have natural resources in abundance. Conservation, wise use, restoration, and development of our natural resources are essential to our national welfare and security.

A hundred years ago, few Americans worried about renewable natural resources. Forests covered vast areas. In many places they were considered a hindrance to agriculture; huge quantities of timber were felled and the logs burned in land clearing. The millions of acres of virgin timber in the South, the Lake States, and the West appeared to be inexhaustible.

Grasses, the plants perhaps most important of all to mankind, clothed the Great Plains and hilly rangelands of the West. So vast were the American grasslands that the pioneers believed it would be centuries before they would be brought under cultivation.

A century ago, wildlife was still so abundant throughout much of America that travelers marveled at the unbelievable numbers. Buffalo, elk, passenger pigeons, prairie chickens, various kinds of waterfowl, and many other game species could be seen in uncounted thousands, even millions.

The nation's wealth of lakes and watercourses provided the natural home for many species of game and food fish. Coastal streams were the spawning grounds for salmon and other sea-run species. The spring runs of shad produced incredible amounts of nourishing food. The offshore, saltwater fishery was still largely unexploited. Water was plentifully available to meet all foreseeable needs throughout most of the eastern and northern regions. Even in the more arid sections of the West, enough water from streams fed by mountain snows and ground waters tapped by wells could be obtained to supply the growing settlements.

Thus, the conservation of natural resources was a new development in our national life. Conservation of certain resources—birdlife, fish, and forests, for example—despite their assumed abundance was advocated by public spirited citizens concerned with the future. The first step taken by the federal government in the interest of a resource was the appointment in 1870 of a U.S. Commissioner of Fish and Fisheries.

Early conservationists were much concerned about the forests. The decimation of timber that resulted from the destructive, wasteful logging methods of the time was readily apparent. Many areas where timber was formerly abundant were now experiencing local shortages.

At the same time, a few sportsmen's organizations began to be concerned about the depletion of game. They began to call for laws that led in time to the establishment of game commissions in several states. The disappearance of passenger pigeons, flocks of which only a few years earlier had clouded the skies, helped to stir the national conscience to thinking about wildlife conservation.

In 1876, the United States Congress authorized the appointment of an agent to study forest conditions. Thus began the federal government's work in forestry which eventually grew into the far-flung activities of the U.S. Forest Service. Around the turn of the century a dynamic young forester named Gifford Pinchot was put in charge of the government's forestry work. He gave the conservation movement a great new impetus. With the support of President Theodore Roosevelt, he helped to broaden the concept of conservation to cover not only the husbanding of resources but their management.

The American Fisheries Society, the first national organization dealing with a specific resource, was founded in 1870. The American Forestry Association, initially concerned mainly with reforestation and forest protection, was organized in 1875. The American Ornithologists' Union was founded in 1883 to promote the protection of game and nongame birds. Other new organizations, concerned with wildlife, water resources, parks and scenic resources, grasslands, and soil conservation, followed.

Many of the early conservationists who found careers in these various fields were men and women of education, usually in the arts and sciences. Before 1900, few had been professionally educated for careers in such employment as fisheries management, silviculture and wildlife management. Such education was not offered in the United States.

Spencer F. Baird, appointed the first United States Commissioner of Fish and Fisheries in 1870, had been a professor of natural history and assistant secretary of the Smithsonian Institution. Franklin B. Hough, appointed in 1876 as the nation's first forestry agent, was a physician. Gifford Pinchot, the country's first technically trained forester, had obtained his education in Europe. C. Hart Merriam, the first head of the biological agency that is now the U.S. Fish and Wildlife Service was educated as a medical doctor.

The rise of natural-resource management as a career, with a foundation in college education, dates from the era of Gifford Pinchot, who showed that resources can be maintained and kept productive permanently. Perhaps fisheries management as a career had earlier beginnings, but the next-oldest career field is forestry. It dates back to 1898, when the first curriculum in forestry at the college level was started at Cornell University. As a profession, forestry may be said to have its origin in the organization of the Society of American Foresters in 1900. Yale, the Universities of Minnesota and Michigan, and a number of other institutions started giving professional training in forestry within the next few years. Today some forty universities and colleges offer four-year courses leading to degrees in forestry. Many of these also offer graduate courses leading to advanced degrees. Many colleges and universities now also have professional courses in range management and wildlife management, and several have established departments of natural resources offering specialized training in several phases of resource management. Training in soil conservation is included in the curriculums of agricultural colleges.

RESOURCE PROBLEMS INCREASE

Conservation work has expanded rapidly and accomplished much in recent years. But the need for conservation has never been greater than it is today. Our resource problems are mounting.

Water, indispensable as it is, is unevenly distributed in the United States. Some regions such as the northeastern and Lake States and western Oregon and Washington have an abundance of water. Other regions such as the arid West are deficient in precipitation. In some localities lack of sufficient water is limiting the possibilities for future growth. Regardless of where water may be locally plentiful, for the nation as a whole the supply for human use is limited. Water safe for drinking without treatment is becoming scarcer in nearly every section of the country. Where watershed lands have been misused, floods have become more frequent and more damaging. Sediment washed from the hillsides is filling streams and reservoirs. The pollution of our streams, the mutilation of watersheds and the erosion of soil have created many problems that must be solved if people are not to suffer from the water shortage.

Hugh Bennett, the foremost soil conservationist of this century, once said, "We Americans ruined more good land than any other nation in history."

The wasteful exploitation of the soil started almost with the first settlers. It has not yet stopped. Millions of acres have been stripped of their forest cover by logging and fire and of their grass cover by overgrazing. They have been drained of fertility by poor farming practices, eroded by floodwaters and winds, and otherwise depleted and abused. In addition, the encroachment of growing cities has removed additional millions of acres from the production of agricultural crops or of trees or grass.

Natural-resource management—as applied to the renewable resources—is the art of making land and water produce adequate yields of products and services for social and economic use. There are numerous specialized lines of work in this field. Game management, according to Aldo Leopold, a pioneer in this field, "is the art of making land produce sustained annual corps of wild game for recreational use." Range management is the science of using rangeland to obtain maximum animal production consistent with perpetuating the land resources. Soil conservation involves the development and application of techniques for the prevention and control of erosion and for the improvement of soil resources. Through watershed management, lands in watershed areas are managed to reduce flooding, stabilize streamflow, and obtain maximum yields of usable water. The Society of American Foresters has defined forestry as "the scientific management of forests for the continuous production of goods and services." The goods and services may include timber and other products, water, wildlife, and recreational opportunities.

Thus the manager of renewable natural resources, educated in the sciences and techniques involved, controls both plant and animal species and their environment for optimum production. Or the manager applies knowledge of natural laws in the maintenance of the soil and water resources upon which other renewable resources depend. Often the controls and manipulation of the environment, when skillfully applied, are hardly visible to the casual observer. Unless the observer is a specialist in the particular field of management under application, he or she might notice no difference between the managed and the unmanaged resource. Two lakes, for example, may appear alike in size, depth, and temperature of water, and they may have other similarities, yet one may be practically devoid of desirable species of fish, while the other, with a well-balanced "food chain," may support an optimum population of game species. One has suffered from misuse. The other is a managed resource.

CAREER WORKERS ARE NEEDED

There is need today for trained, capable workers in all fields of management. As our increasing population and expanding industries make greater and greater demands on our resources, the need will grow.

Who should choose a career in conservation? As might be expected, a liking for the outdoors leads many young persons to conservation activities. Much of the work of resource management, of course, must be done out in the fields or forests, often in places remote from the conveniences of urban living. The happy and successful conservation worker, therefore, is likely to be one who enjoys such an environment and who is resourceful and self-reliant enough to feel at home in wild areas. Sufficient stamina and strength for outdoor work are usually needed.

Whether employment is with a public agency or in private enterprise, the conservation worker is serving the public good. He or she should have an interest in the social welfare, a desire to help community and nation, to contribute to human progress.

Originality, imagination, determination, and patience are desirable assets. Good character, a sense of responsibility, honesty, and reliability are as important in conservation work as in any other career. Some of the professional organizations in the conservation field have adopted ethical standards with which all members are expected to conform.

Natural-resource management has become so technical that a person not technically or professionally educated in a specialty has little opportunity for developing a career in the field. The first educational requirement is sound grounding in the basic sciences, particularly in mathematics, economics, chemistry, physics, and ecology. A good knowledge of English and especially training in grammatical speech and writing are essential.

The person educated in the basic sciences only is not prepared for a professional career in resource management. Additional education should be obtained in a professional curriculum, such as fisheries, forestry, range management, watershed management, or wildlife management. It should be emphasized that however sincere a young person may be in his or her dedication to improving the environment, dedication alone is not enough for a full-time career in resource management, except in a subordinate position or a vocational type of employment.

If one chooses a career in conservation, how will one prepare for it? Nearly every college or university offers instruction in the biological sciences which are the background of most resource-management work. Courses in English and other subjects also are available, and these have value in conservation. They help to widen one's knowledge and to improve one's ability to think clearly and intelligently.

More specialized training in resource management is available at forestry schools and in range-management, wildlife-management, and other natural-resource curriculums offered at a number of universities and colleges. Most students desire to go further into specializations in graduate studies to advanced degrees. Various fields of specialization are described in later chapters of this book.

Scholarships are available to students for undergraduate and graduate work. Some are for general, others for specialized studies. Employees in many conservation agencies often are given the opportunity to obtain further on-the-job training and to pursue special studies in their particular line of work.

Employment opportunities in natural-resource management are constantly expanding. Several agencies of the federal government carry on programs in conservation. The larger ones include the Forest Service and Soil Conservation Service of the Department of Agriculture, the Bureau of Land Management, the Fish and Wildlife Service, and the National Park Service of the Department of the Interior. The National Marine Fisheries Service of the Department of Commerce has many biologists working with marine and estuarine resources. The Defense Department has undertaken the management of forests, wildlife and other resources on military and naval reservations. Employment in the federal agencies generally is career service; new employees enter in the lower-grade positions and, as they gain experience and capability, are promoted to positions of greater responsibility.

The conservation departments, fish and game departments, forestry departments, and agricultural extension services of the various states also offer opportunities for employment. In most states these also are career services, governed by the states' civil service or merit system rules. Many counties and municipalities need persons educated in resource management to administer community parks, forests, and watersheds.

Teaching positions in colleges and universities are most often obtained by those who have earned advanced degrees. Many secondary schools are also seeking persons educated in conservation or in the related sciences. Resource-management specialists find employment, too, in a number of national and regional conservation organizations such as citizens' and industrial associations.

Many persons educated in resource management find employment in private enterprise. For example, utility companies, timber companies, and pulp and paper manufacturers employ foresters for the management and protection of their woodland holdings and for related work. Other concerns with forest land or other wildland holdings sometimes seek resource managers. Some resource managers go into private consulting work, usually after experience in government or industry employment.

Some resource-management specialists with experience in this country are finding assignments overseas. They serve as consultants to foreign governments or as participants in American foreign-aid or United Nations programs to help other countries with their resource problems.

Other professionals and scientists whose primary education is in other fields are finding interesting and rewarding work in resources and environmental activities. Generally, they are persons with special concerns and knowledge in conservation. Among these—and this is only a partial list—are agricultural, civil, and sanitary engineers, arboriculturists, chemists, computer scientists, ecologists, economists, editors and writers, entomologists, geologists, historians, horticulturists, landscape architects, mathematicians, pathologists, physicists, toxicologists, and numerous others. Educational preparation needed for these professions is described in other reference books and career manuals that can be found in public libraries and some high school libraries.

A person whose primary career objective is money probably should seek other careers, although salaries in the resource-management professions are generally comparable with those in other professions requiring similar educational preparation. Retirement annuities, medical insurance, and other benefits are provided by the federal government and most other employing agencies.

There are other rewards. Most conservation workers find their work pleasant and interesting. They enjoy the associations with others whose interests are similar, whose motives are usually unselfish and public-spirited. And there is real satisfaction in doing work that is needed and worthwhile, work that is contributing to the welfare of others, the nation and the world.

2 Environmnetal Conservation

HUGH O. CANHAM

Environmental conservation is one of the oldest and one of the newest areas of human activity. Man has always wondered about, investigated and attempted to control the world in which he lives. It is only recently, however, that we have begun to understand the intricate relationships that determine our environment—the linkage of geology with economics and politics.

Environmental conservation is not the clearly defined profession that forestry or wildlife management is. It is not a discipline such as biology or physics. Instead, environmental conservation can be thought of as an approach to problems, a viewpoint, an interdisciplinary area of study. It is defined as the rational use of natural resources and human resources to provide a high quality of living for people. Many activities are involved, including the preservation of certain fragile natural areas, and the modification of others. Today's needs must be given attention and plans made for the future. Resources must be managed to meet a wide range of human wants.

Historically, concern for use of natural resources arose in response to immediate problems. Early humans in the postglacial period faced self-preservation in a hostile world. They were nomads, moving when local resources gave out. With the development of agriculture, small communities were formed and people settled in one place. It soon became evident that local supplies of wood, soil, and water had to be carefully managed.

The Sumerians, 3000 years ago in Mesopotamia, developed highly efficient systems for controlling silt in the Tigris and Euphrates Rivers. They distributed water through elaborate canals for use on farms. Large quantities of human resources were applied in an advanced political system giving them a high quality of living through conservation of their natural resources. But the breakdown of the social environment by invading armies led to drastic changes in the biological and physical environment. The rich fertile river valley deteriorated into a desert with few inhabitants, a dramatic lesson in environmental conservation.

Early Greek writers saw the link between animal wastes and crop fertilization and advocated use of manures to improve food yields. The Romans, and later the northern Europeans, developed agricultural systems in harmony with their environment. These early developments were in response to local problems, although the results were often carried over to succeeding generations.

European settlers in North America brought with them the heritage of conservation. Early in colonial history, laws were enacted prohibiting burning of forests at certain times of the year. In Pennsylvania, William Penn required one acre of woods left for every five acres cleared. Other laws were enacted in the 1700s and early 1800s.

In the late 1800s, however, a great conservation movement spread across the entire United States. It was not born from immediate local shortages or problems that characterized earlier efforts. Instead, there was a farsighted view to possible future needs. People such as G. P. Marsh, John Muir, B. E. Fernow, and Gifford Pinchot were looking forward hundreds of years when they pushed for wilderness preservation, national parks, and public forests. This view to the future has dominated conservation thinking since then.

Starting in the 1960s a new wave of environmentalism swept the country. Even though it is similar to the conservation era of 100 years ago, the present era differs in significant ways. The emphasis is on a systems view, studying the interactions among the various elements of the total environment. Urban systems with highly complex social and biological components, the home of most Americans, are a major focus of the new environmental conservation. In our highly industrialized society, the systems view now extends from basic natural resources through manufacturing processes to the consumer, and back to natural resources.

This environmental conservationist is gathering information on field conditions affecting the environment. He is measuring snow depth to determine later water runoff. (Photo by U.S. Forest Service.)

Solutions to the problems faced by our modern society require two things—professionals assembled from many different disciplines to analyze problems and develop solutions, and an enlightened citizenry expressing its desires in a rational and intelligent manner. Environmental conservation as a field of study aids in fulfilling both requirements.

EDUCATION IN ENVIRONMENTAL CONSERVATION

Education in environmental conservation serves three purposes: (1) to provide the specialist with an integrative, or systems, view of the environment; (2) to provide persons with a general basis for more specific advanced study in a particular discipline; (3) to develop intelligent citizens. Thus, environmental conservation might be termed the "liberal arts" of natural resources.

Unlike other subject areas in this book, the field of environmental conservation does not have a standard educational curriculum. College programs in this field go by a variety of names, such as environmental studies, resource conservation, environmental management, or environmental conservation. Students usually put their academic programs together under faculty guidance.

The most important educational guideline for the student is to know the underlying theory and principles in both natural and social sciences which give rise to issues and which provide the basis for solutions to problems in environmental conservation. Courses should be completed in biology, chemistry, physics, geology, economics, geography, political science, psychology, and sociology. Communication skills and skills in mathematics and statistics are necessary.

Many colleges offer advanced courses in specific fields with the subject matter applied to broad environmental issues. For the general citizen a few of these courses may suffice. Some typical courses include environmental economics, natural resource economics, conservation of natural resources, environmental biology, environmental law, and systems oriented seminars led by interdisciplinary teams of students and faculty.

Today a number of colleges and universities offer a major in environmental conservation. In some schools a student must complete a major in a traditional discipline in order to complete a second or joint major in environmental conservation. In other cases a student can major solely in environmental studies. In many programs two alternatives are available, one emphasizing the biological and physical sciences, the other emphasizing social sciences. The student can then obtain depth of knowledge in a specific part of the environment for either post-graduation employment or for graduate study.

In either case the basic courses described earlier are necessary. Applied courses at the junior and senior level should include at least advanced resource economics, applied ecology, and soil science. The political arena in which public policy is decided must also be understood.

Graduate degrees, usually a master of science, are becoming prevalent in this area. Advanced study requires a good academic record, adequate preparation in biological sciences, social sciences, and quantitative techniques, and above all a sincere desire to pursue some area in depth. Fields related to environmental conservation at the graduate level include resource economics, public administration, regional planning, wildlife management, forest management, open space management and watershed management.

Courses in environmental law or natural resources law are available. However, an in-depth curriculum in law requires three years of study beyond the bachelor's level. Lawyers specializing in environmental law often combine study in a natural resources field with their legal background.

Financial assistance for education in environmental conservation is comparable to other fields of study. Undergraduates are eligible for federal loans, and many colleges have scholarships. Opportunities exist for limited work with faculty members on research, usually for upperclass students with some skills. At the graduate level, teaching assistantships are offered to some students. Knowledge of some specific subject matter and the ability to work with students are needed to qualify for these limited assistantships. Research grants offer other means of financial support.

PERSONAL QUALIFICATIONS

Education alone does not produce people qualified to work in the field of environmental conservation. Individual personal abilities combined with formal training will give society a useful professional. One of the most important personal characteristics is the ability to see things in a balanced perspective.

The farmer needs to make a living, and the urban resident needs the food the farmer produces, yet laws severely restricting normal farming operations get passed in state legislatures. The fisherman wants clean water, the industrial water user may return his effluent to the river cleaner than when it was withdrawn, yet regulations are imposed limiting the number of fish that may be taken and requiring further water treatment by firms. The environmental conservationist must be able to understand these complex issues and to see all sides. The conservationist must realize that there are no single solutions but that compromise is necessary.

The ability to work comfortably within a group is a trait of those who are successful in this area. To solve today's complex issues requires a team effort, both in research and decisionmaking.

Effective communication, written and oral, is another requisite. People who engage in environmental conservation must communicate with the public. Public speaking, news releases and informational reports, such as environmental impact statements, are all used. Other professionals, supervisors and colleagues, will be in touch on a daily basis. With the varying backgrounds of people in the field it is important to be able to explain a technical subject in plain language.

The environmental conservationist must be able to synthesize. Many different disciplines and points of view must be brought together. Attention to detailed analysis is important, yet the generalist in environmental conservation must also be pragmatic and put things together in a way that will lead to a rational decision.

There are many unknowns in the environment. The professional today is being challenged by the public, and by other professionals. The field of environmental conservation is particularly subject to criticism. The aspiring professional must be able to accept criticism and make constructive use of it. At the same time one must be tolerant and respect the viewpoint of others.

Above all, in a rapidly developing and amorphous field such as environmental conservation one must have a continued interest in professional development. The issues of tomorrow are not those of today.

EMPLOYMENT

Employment for people with education in environmental conservation is available in many different forms—in private industry, as consultants, or with public agencies, foundations and associations. Employers are often interested in hiring persons for certain specific, immediate tasks. Hence, there is the need for some specialization in education. Very few people are hired as the overall planner or decision maker, and few have the phrase "environmental conservation" in their job title. They rise to the position through education, experience, and abilities.

Private industry, once thought of as the "bad guy of the environment," is demonstrating a genuine interest in, and commitment to, consideration of the entire environment. Power companies, for example, have offices of environmental analysis or environmental impact. These offices hire biologists, economists, and engineers concerned with the total effect of proposed power generation plants or transmission lines on the environment. They gather information on things such as water conditions, land use, the economy, and topography. This information is analyzed by the environmental group and reports are prepared for company action or for securing permits from government agencies.

Pulp and paper companies and integrated chemical producers are two other industrial employers of environmentally trained people. A major concern of these companies is the discharge of waste effluents. Interdisciplinary teams study the biological and social impacts of such discharges and the costs and benefits of waste reduction.

Private consultants prepare plans and analyze impacts on the environment of proposed actions. They may prepare reports for private firms or for public agencies. Employment for consultants varies with the rise and fall of workloads and the shifting job market.

Public agencies were originally the biggest employers for all natural resources professions. With the passage of the National Environmental Policy Act in 1969 public employment opportunities for people trained in environmental conservation surged upward. In recent years, however, there has been a tendency at both the federal and state level to cut back or stabilize the number of employees.

General training in environmental conservation coupled with a specialty provides skills for employment with federal agencies such as the Soil Conservation Service, Forest Service, Fish and Wildlife Service, Environmental Protection Agency, Federal Highway Agency, and Nuclear Regulatory Commission. Many of these jobs are under the federal Civil Service and have specific educational and experience prerequisites. Temporary employment or work at a technician level is a way for the young college graduate to begin a career.

State agencies are also looking for generalists with usable specialties: forestry, sanitary engineering, wildlife biology, or resource economics. Typical state agencies hiring people in the field include public service commissions, state highway or public works departments, parks departments, conservation or natural resource departments and planning agencies.

Work for federal and state agencies often involves data gathering under field conditions, analysis and report writing and the review of plans prepared by others. Increasingly, state employees are involved in public hearings and litigation over land-use changes, utility rights-of-way, and water quality.

State, county, and metropolitan planning agencies offer interesting employment opportunities. (Community development or urban renewal agencies are included in this category.) These jobs do not all come under civil service provisions, and the number of positions is somewhat limited.

Finally, foundations, clubs, and associations provide some unusual employment opportunities for people with training in environmental conservation. The number of openings is small, but the work is exciting and varied. A major activity of many organizations is interpretation of complex environmental material for the public through television programs, brochures, and nature center activities. There may be extensive work with volunteer groups. Fund raising is often a prime concern.

Women and minority groups are not discriminated against in environmental conservation. An employer is interested in hiring the person with a sincere interest in the job, knowledge of systems at work in the environment, skills to find a particular role and ability to get along with other people.

The major employment obstacle at present is the intense competition for a limited number of jobs in environmental conservation. The field is broad and vaguely defined. Jobs may not be as well defined as in other fields described in this book. Indeed, it is often the well trained specialist with additional graduate training in environmental conservation who will be most sought after.

COMPENSATION AND REWARDS

A person receives from a career what he or she puts into it. Exciting and rewarding careers in environmental conservation exist for serious individuals committed to development of a balanced, high quality of living for all.

Financial returns will allow a person to enjoy a modest living. One should not, however, enter the field expecting high income. Salaries are competitive with other career opportunities in natural resources but definitely below engineering, medicine, and law.

Private industry and public agencies generally start out at similar salary levels. Advanced positions in industry usually pay more than public employment.

Initially, temporary employment at a subprofessional level may be necessary. Such jobs should not be overlooked. If the pay is low the main reward is experience and the opportunity for advancement to higher status.

There are many nonfinancial benefits from working in environmental conservation. It is a subject of much concern. People everywhere want to know more about their world. One's colleagues are usually stimulating and congenial. Working on a team with different professionals enlarges an individual's perspective.

The environment is a perplexing system. Changes may be subtle and extremely long term. On the other hand swift, often dramatic, unpredictable events take place. Much is still unknown, and technology and public policy bring new developments each day. Caught in such a dynamic, intricate system the individual may become disheartened. One knows, however, that he or she is working in an area that has occupied man's attention since the dawn of history—the environment in, on, and surrounding our small spaceship earth.

3 Soil Conservation

VERLON K. VRANA and WALTER E. JESKE

The soil conservationist helps people care for their environment by:

1. Understanding how to use the land according to its capabilities so that it is not damaged.
2. Keeping the soil productive in order to provide food and the other life-support needs for humans and the many creatures with which they share the Earth.
3. Managing resources to improve the quality of water available for human and wildlife needs.
4. Protecting the soil as the basic natural resource necessary for maintaining a high quality environment.

Soil conservation is interdisciplinary. To prevent and solve practical problems in resource management and land use requires knowledge and skills from many of the physical, biological, and social sciences.

In this chapter "soil conservationist" is used as a general term to include workers trained in such fields as soil science, agronomy, range conservation, biology, geology, landscape design, wildlife management, forestry, botany, and plant materials testing. It also includes workers trained as hydraulic, drainage, agricultural, irrigation, and civil engineers. Professionals from each of these fields have an important place in resource management and land use.

A district conservationist for the Soil Conservation Service uses a surveying instrument to obtain precise data for use in designing conservation practices. (Photo by Soil Conservation Service.)

All people depend on land and water wherever they may live. People in suburbs and cities build on the land and depend for food on farms, ranches, and orchards where other people work with soil, water, and related resources in producing food for the nation.

To the early settlers in this country, the land appeared limitless. It was easy to leave worn-out acres and move on to new land. Less than a hundred years later—by the mid-1800s—there was no more new land. Farmers sought new ways of cultivating and planting to keep soil from washing away and to maintain the productivity of the land. But millions of acres in the Southeast were already gullied and wasted by uncontrolled erosion that clogged streams with sediment.

It was not until the 1930s, when thousands of farmers in the Great Plains were driven from their land by drought, soil erosion, and dust storms, that a national program of soil and water conservation began with the establishment of the Soil Conservation Service in 1935 in the U.S. Department of Agriculture.

The immediate tasks of the new agency were to help restore lands eroded by wind and water and to help farmers protect and maintain lands in use for food and fiber production.

By 1940, most states had enacted laws that enabled citizens to create local soil conservation districts as legal entities for the purpose of helping solve soil and water conservation problems. Through such districts, public and private assistance was made available for applying soil and water conservation practices.

Research at land grant colleges on effects of soil erosion and methods to control it combined with efforts by soil conservation districts soon broadened the scope of soil and water programs.

On the outskirts of cities, housing developments and the construction of airports and shopping centers laid bare hundreds of acres to wind and water erosion. Planners and developers discovered that erosion control measures designed to protect farmland worked equally well on lands in other uses. In time, the soil and water conservation program literally changed the face of America.

The soil conservation movement also helped change the way people thought about their environment. Farmers, businessmen, bankers and others no longer regarded land solely as a commodity to be bought and sold, but thought of it as the base of their life-support system. Further, soil conservation helped citizens become aware of their responsibility for taking care of natural resources.

Later, other responsibilities were added by law to the original soil and water conservation program, such as technical and financial help for watershed protection and flood prevention, resource conservation and development on a multicounty basis, and an accelerated survey of soils to determine their basic characteristics.

Today, soil conservationists have a part in such projects as land and resource inventorying and monitoring by satellite; working with local leaders to develop multicounty resource conservation and development projects; helping governmental officials and planners devise regulations and set standards for erosion control; helping individuals and agencies with wildlife habitat improvement; providing aid to cooperative snow survey programs that furnish information for water supply forecasting in the arid states of the West.

New technologies, expanding land use demands, and changing attitudes of citizens toward economic, social, and political aspects of resource management directly affect the work of soil conservationists and the skills they must bring to the job. But the future of soil and water conservation will continue to hinge on helping people analyze and understand their environmental problems, find workable solutions to those problems, and consider carefully the consequences of their decisions on any natural resource issue.

EDUCATION

College training with a degree in a physical or natural science is required for most professional careers in soil conservation. The soil conservationist may be a soil scientist by training, which means concentration on soil classification and survey, soil microbiology, soil management, soil chemistry, and other studies related directly to the soil.

The conservationist may also be trained in one or more related fields:

1. *Agronomy*, including studies of soil management, weed control, crop production, tillage, and many other facets of managing plants for food, feed, and fiber production purposes.
2. *Biology*, including aspects of biochemistry, botany, zoology, ecology, entomology, and specialized studies, such as soil microbiology, plant pathology, genetics, and cell biology.
3. *Range management*, including basic botany and ecology as well as specialized work in soils, plant physiology and pathology, water management, and utilization of plants by animals.

Many agencies and private businesses employ conservation engineers—agricultural, irrigation, hydraulic, and civil. There is also some demand for conservation engineers specializing in fluid mechanics, thermodynamics, functional design of agricultural structures, and land and water resource engineering.

Not all jobs in soil conservation require a college degree. There will continue to be more and more opportunities for paraprofessionals, individual with an associate degree, usually earned in two-year programs at technical or community colleges. There are also opportunities for individuals with a high school diploma. Paraprofessionals generally work as conservation aides. They may gather data needed for conservation planning, assist with timber stand improvement, stake out contour lines, perform construction inspections on conservation projects, and many other tasks dealing directly with proper use and care of the land.

There are no sex, racial, or ethnic barriers to a conservation career. In some geographical areas, it is an advantage to be able to speak a foreign language—Spanish, for example—in working with land owners and users.

Women are entering every conservation field in increasing numbers. Equal opportunity programs in government and in private organizations have opened many doors in technical fields to both women and minorities.

Today's student has a variety of electives not formerly offered in preparing for resource management jobs. For example, there are courses in environmental assessment and impact, techniques of environmental systems analysis, and supervisory training.

Communication is an essential part of any soil conservationist's job and should be included as part of formal training.

Not only must the conservationist get the message across to land users at different levels of education, but he or she must be able to speak clearly and use audiovisual techniques with skill and ease.

Conservation careers depend on continuing education and training. As new problems and issues arise and new techniques in resource management are developed, the professional soil conservationist must keep abreast by taking special courses, participating in professional societies, and continuously studying the literature related to resource use and management.

Many federal agencies and private firms maintain career development programs with training sessions scheduled periodically for people working in different fields and programs. Some agencies also offer home study courses, including refresher studies in basic science.

Not only do conservationists need to keep up to date in technological fields, but also they must understand the economic, cultural, and political climate of the times. Government agencies as well as private employers also offer opportunities for graduate study in technical and administrative fields.

Students can sometimes get a headstart through work-learning programs and internships. For example, through the Civil Service Commission, the Soil Conservation Service (SCS) sponsors a student trainee program open to college freshmen, sophomores and juniors. Many accredited colleges and universities have a cooperative education program, which is frequently used by private industries that employ natural resource specialists. By working in the field during vacations, a student becomes prepared to step into a full-time professional job upon graduation. Work experience often helps students focus on the specific job they want and is useful in planning college studies realistically.

To qualify for the SCS Student Training Program, the candidate should be majoring in soil conservation, engineering, soils, biology, forestry, range or farm management, agricultural economics, wildlife management, animal husbandry, or another conservation-related field.

The student trainee can expect a variety of learning experiences:

1. Working with soil conservationists in applying onsite conservation measures, such as terracing, stripcropping, conservation tillage, contour farming, and establishing vegetation for erosion control; solving irrigation and drainage problems and interpreting soil survey information for different land uses.
2. Working with professionals to help local leaders make and carry out community natural resource and land use plans; assist with the organization and assembly of data for environmental impact statements.
3. Assisting range conservationists to help ranchers determine the suitability of their land for native forage or to develop conservation plans for improving range productivity for livestock and wildlife; assembling data and giving advice on how to improve range conditions, control poisonous or noxious plants, and plan water resource development for livestock and wildlife.
4. Working with a biologist to improve wildlife habitat or with a forester on woodland conservation management.

The Soil Conservation Society of America (SCSA) offers scholarships to undergraduates who have completed two years of study at an accredited college or university. Scholarship winners have studied in such fields as agronomy, soil science, range management, forestry, geography, and wildlife management. Students are free to chose their area of concentration as long as it is related to conservation of natural resources. Information and applications can be obtained from local chapters of SCSA or from its national headquarters at 7515 N.E. Ankeny Road, Ankeny, Iowa, 50021.

Selecting a suitable college can be a confusing task, but information on various colleges and universities can be found in college catalogs and course descriptions. Most high school, college, and community libraries have a broad array of materials on specific educational offerings at colleges.

An especially good means of getting reliable information about colleges is by talking with professionals now working in the field, recent graduates of various colleges, and representatives of colleges that visit your high school.

Some questions you might want answered either by mail or during an interview are:

1. What are the entrance requirements? Some colleges demand specific kinds of credentials.
2. What are the specific courses required for a degree in the student's fields of interest relating to conservation? Check the list of courses and make sure they are offered regularly.
3. What are the costs? When comparing costs, one must be sure to include tuition, books, living costs, parking fees, student activity fees, and laboratory or special equipment fees.
4. Is financial aid available through state, federal, or private programs or student loans? One should get all the details and read them carefully.

PERSONAL QUALIFICATIONS

The most important qualification for a career in soil conservation, besides technical know-how, is the ability to work with people—people of all ages and backgrounds, all economic and education levels.

For example, the soil conservationist may work with school administrators, teachers, and students to provide technical help for an environmental studies program. Colleges and universities frequently invite soil conservationists to lecture in many different courses, to work with undergraduates on environmental education, or to help plan outdoor classrooms.

Conservationists often work with individuals and groups that have little or no understanding of natural resources and the ways in which soil, water, and plants are interrelated. The conservationist must be able to discuss the immediate problem, present some alternative solutions along with their likely consequences, and explain the basics of ecosystem processes—all in plain English.

Much soil conservation work is done in the field and requires ordinary good health and stamina. Gathering data for soil surveys and helping develop conservation plans for farms, ranches, and other land uses will mean tramping through fields, woodlands, and wildlife areas. Field work may include measuring slopes, providing guidance on use of conservation methods, or designing grass waterways.

The soil conservationist is not likely to be involved in research per se, but it is a good idea to be familiar with research procedures in order to evaluate and apply the findings of investigations. Time in the office is spent on work ranging from preparation of conservation plans, writing reports, analyzing data for different purposes, to public information work, and providing responses to questions from land owners and users.

Geographically, the conservationist's job may be almost anywhere in the nation. It may be in a small town or in the suburbs of a large city. It may be in the arid West, in the Mississippi Delta, or in the rich farmlands of the Midwest. Conservationists need to be active members of the community as well as professional workers. They should be sensitive to local customs and history and willing to look at social and cultural aspects of conservation problems.

EMPLOYMENT

Federal agencies employ the largest numbers of soil conservationists and other natural resource specialists. But there is a growing market for professionals by private industries, such as oil companies, commercial timber producers, surface mining companies, building contractors, large farms and ranches, and other industries that depend on use and management of soil and other resources.

Regional planning commissions, riverbasin commissions, and all state departments of natural resources employ conservationists trained in a variety of fields—wildlife managers, soil scientists, water management experts, and so on. Other employment opportunities are with conservation organizations that conduct research or develop study areas for birds and other wildlife and for native plants.

Soil and water conservation districts, as special purpose units of government, are responsible for making long-range programs that focus on finding solutions to local natural resource problems. Though SCS and other federal and state government agencies provide technical services to districts for conservation purposes, they may need additional personnel in some instances. Some districts have hired qualified people to review the adequacy of required erosion and sediment control plans for subdivision and other large-scale earth disturbing projects. Others hire environmental education consultants. Still others hire specialists in administrative or other areas.

As sponsors of small watershed projects or resource conservation and development areas, conservation districts may employ soil conservationists and other professionals.

Soil conservationists and other resource specialists prepare range site and range condition maps, woodland and wildlife suitability maps, and provide information on appropriate conservative use of different plants. These include grasses, trees, and wildlife food and cover.

Technical assistance in designing, laying out, and checking the construction and maintenance of dams, terraces, and other structures may be provided through district programs. On the edges of cities, some of the work of the conservationist, in cooperation with the district, includes suggesting guidelines for controlling erosion along highway rights of way, and in subdivisions, shopping centers, airports and other areas. Providing information about use and conservation management of soil and water resources for housing, recreation, waste disposal, road construction, and other needs is part of the soil conservationist's responsibilities.

Under Section 208 of the Water Pollution Control Act Amendments of 1972, the Environmental Protection Agency has turned to conservation districts for leadership in identifying nonpoint pollution sources. In states where sediment control on private lands is mandated by law, districts may employ inspectors to monitor performance at construction sites and other land-use projects.

Population growth, affluence, and mobility are bringing about new problems of resource use and intensifying the need for conservation measures to protect the land.

Suburban home developments have removed many acres of prime farmland. In the search for homesites, some people have built on steep hillsides where soil slippage has resulted in severe damage to houses, on flood plains where overflowing rivers have swept away homes, and in arid areas where inadequate water supplies are a continuing problem.

More people are building vacation or second homes in rural or wooded areas without proper planning for waste disposal or on soils unsuited to the use of septic tanks.

More speedboats and other recreation craft on lakes, reservoirs, and rivers have led to wave erosion of banks and shorelines.

These are some of the problems that must be tackled by soil conservationists and other natural resource specialists through planning and the application of appropriate conservation management systems.

Soil scientists, agronomists, and engineers are increasingly involved in solid waste disposal and agricultural waste management. Solid wastes must be buried where they do not contaminate water resources. Disposal of animal wastes from farms and feedlots requires the help of soil scientists and other specialists to plan management systems that minimize adverse impacts on water quality.

Several federal agencies provide technical assistance in natural resource management to foreign countries. Hundreds of soil conservationists and other specialists are assigned each year to nations in the Middle East, Africa, South America, Central America, and other locations. Foreign assignments are coordinated through the Agency for International Development in the U.S. Department of State.

COMPENSATION AND REWARDS

Soil conservation is professional service for meeting the environmental and economic needs of people through wise use and protection of natural resources.

It means tackling tough problems that require not only scientific know-how but also understanding, imagination, and persistence.

Salary scales in government agencies are comparable with those in similar professional fields, and salaries in private employment are comparable with those paid by government for similar levels of responsibility. Generally, higher salaries come with increases in scope of responsibility. A soil research position at a university might pay a high salary, but such positions require advanced degrees.

Soil conservationists are aware of the past and its meaning for the present. Most important, they look to the future, working for renewal of woodlands, improving wildlife habitat, maintaining the productivity of farms and ranches, managing growth in suburban areas, and minimizing the adverse impacts of humans on soil, water, and related natural resources.

By helping children plant a tree or plan a conservation learning trail, the soil conservationist is touching the future of the nation.

Personal satisfaction with a job or a career has no price tag. In rectifying past mistakes, in helping people make their communities a better place to live, and in preserving and increasing the productive capacity of the soil, the conservationist serves all Americans and the welfare of humanity.

4 Outdoor Recreation

GRANT W. SHARPE

A young person at the career planning stage will probably not be old enough to remember when people used to ask, "a career in outdoor recreation? You mean you can get a job fishing and hunting for the rest of your life?" Times have changed. Young people today are well aware of the importance of leisure and recreation in their lives and are sophisticated enough to know that the lands and waters which support recreation need knowledgeable people to plan, manage, and interpret them.

A few decades ago most used to go camping to hunt and fish. Now persons of all ages seek the out-of-doors for many reasons, sometimes just to be camping, but more often to camp as a base for hiking or trail riding, horseback riding, swimming, water skiing, or some other leisure pursuit. The woods are full of people seeking enjoyment, and people who are trying to keep the multitudes from harming the resources upon which their good times depend. More people with more leisure mean more problems, but also more careers in helping to keep it all under control.

Outdoor recreation usually takes place on large tracts of land managed by some government agency—city, county, state, or federal. Here is where most outdoor recreation graduates find employment. There is an increasing number of smaller private recreation areas, such as dude ranches and commercial campgrounds, but these do not

33

A National Park Service ranger's horse is admired by young visitors to Yosemite National Park. (Photo by National Park Service.)

usually hire outdoor recreation professionals, except perhaps in the planning stage. A few industrial forests, private utilities, and mining companies with large ownership provide recreation on their lands but the employment opportunities for recreation graduates are small.

Persons interested in recreation have two routes they may follow. One is *outdoor* recreation, which depends on some particular resource, or a combination of natural resources, such as lakes, rivers, forests, mountains, deserts, or oceans. The resource often dictates the location and type of activity. The training for outdoor recreation specialists usually takes place in a *resource-oriented* college, and this is the kind of recreation career this chapter deals with.

The other kind of recreation is *activity-oriented* rather than resource-oriented. This recreation specialist can organize games, teach sports, lead dancing, and in other ways keep diverse groups interested and happy. These people are often called program or leadership recreationists. Employment is largely with municipal and county park and recreation departments. Institutions such as public health centers, nursing homes, and prisons are hiring more people in therapeutic recreation. Many obtain employment as recreation specialists in a civilian capacity in the armed forces. These activity specialists receive their training in the department of physical education, or a parks and recreation department, or other municipal-related curriculum. Some colleges in recent years have attempted to combine their resource-oriented recreation curriculums with the activity-oriented programs.

Let us return to outdoor recreation. Natural resources provide the scene and inspiration for a great variety of recreational offerings, including hunting and fishing, camping and picnicking, walking, hiking, and climbing, driving various types of vehicles in outdoor settings, boating and other water sports, winter sports, photography, painting, and numerous forms of nature study. Space to do all of these things is limited, and these activities are often in conflict with each other or with other land uses cited elsewhere in this book. Therefore, it becomes necessary for professionally trained planners and managers to accommodate these uses in a manner causing least conflict with each other and the least damage to the land or water base. The interpreter also has a role in preservation and accommodation through the education of the visitors.

Ever since the early state and national parks were established in the late 1800s and early 1900s there has been a demand for people trained in outdoor recreation. Because of increases in population, leisure time, and incomes, improved travel facilities, and an awakening of environmental concerns, millions of citizens in North America annually participate in resource recreation activities, and their participation increases annually, creating an even greater need for professionals in the field.

EDUCATIONAL REQUIREMENTS

A four-year college degree is preferred, although it is not absolutely essential with certain agencies. Two-year technician programs are available at some colleges. Competition is keen for the better jobs, however, and those students with bachelors degrees may have a greater opportunity for advancement. A four-year degree is standard for most entry level federal positions. Most state and some county park systems also require a bachelor's degree. Some county and state agencies permit substitution of a year of park-related experience for one year of college.

The degree should be in forest recreation, outdoor recreation, park management, or a closely related field. These are curriculums intended to train people for *specific positions* in outdoor recreation. Because of the way civil service specifications are written, however, people with degrees in other professions are often qualified for these same positions. Some agencies prefer people with a police science background to assist in their law enforcement and vandalism problems. Landscape architects are often hired to work as park planners. Positions in the management field may require someone with a background in business administration or political science. For some interpretive positions botanists, zoologists, geologists, historians, archeologists and anthropologists may qualify. Graduates in wildlife sciences, forest management, engineering, and similar curriculums often qualify for general recreation positions. The recreation field is varied and the individual would be well advised to look into specific agency requirements.

Those going into outdoor recreation teaching or research will usually seek a doctorate, although, in a few instances, a master's degree may be adequate.

GETTING PRACTICAL EXPERIENCE

Because summer is the major recreation season, jobs are normally plentiful for students seeking summer employment. Most agencies give recreation majors preference in seasonal employment. Also, when filling permanent jobs, most agencies prefer applicants who have had a summer or two of park or other outdoor recreation experience, preferably with them. This way the agency has had a chance to evaluate the employee, and similarly the employee has a realistic picture of the agency. Some colleges with outdoor recreation programs will place a job searcher where jobs are located to notified students about job opportunities. Frequently, a college will have an intern program, either volunteer or compulsory, in which students may also gain experience. It is obviously to a student's advantage to work seasonally in recreation while in college. In a competitive world the man or woman with experience and a good work rating will have a better chance for a permanent job than a person with no experience. By the same reasoning, it will be advantageous to have sought outdoor recreation experience in jobs before entering the university, such as park aid, trail crew, camp counselor, fire suppression crew, or volunteer work of any kind in this field.

CORE CURRICULUMS IN OUTDOOR RECREATION

The four years of a basic resource-oriented recreation program contain essentially the following:

1. Biology
2. Physical sciences
3. Natural sciences
4. Social sciences
5. Natural resources
6. Communications (speaking and writing)
7. Administration and policy
8. Electives

The mix varies with colleges and universities. If the curriculum is in a forestry college, the natural resources courses may be given more emphasis. Some curriculums provide for specialization, enabling a student to concentrate on one of several fields such as recreation management, recreation planning, or interpretation.

In the management area a student is concerned with overall business of maintaining and running a park or recreation complex. The *manager* is the person in charge, and his or her concern is record keeping, personnel management, fiscal and legal matters, public opinion, public relations, organization theory, law enforcement, fire control, maintenance, and conflict resolution.

The *recreation planner* is concerned with the design and location of park facilities and must be knowledgeable in sanitation and water systems, trail and road standards, campground and picnic area layout, interpretive needs, and the impacts of various recreational activities on the park environment. Writing impact assessments has become part of the planner's job.

The *interpretive specialist* works with the park manager in encouraging the visitor to acquire an understanding and an appreciation of the park's cultural and natural resources. This person is also concerned with using interpretation as a device for reducing human impact on a fragile or overused resource. Interpreters must have an understanding not only of natural and cultural resources, but also of communications techniques, park policy, and the social sciences. Vital skills include photography, public speaking ability, and working with interpretive devices.

On the other hand, a student may follow a *general program* for four years, and then specialize in one of these three areas, or another specialty, at the fifth year or graduate level.

Most resource-oriented colleges offer at least one or two courses in outdoor recreation. Others offer entire curriculums on the subject. College entrants should inquire about these programs.

Another factor to consider is the number of graduates a college turns out yearly. Some colleges do not restrict enrollment in outdoor recreation and turn out large numbers of graduates who flood the job market. When investigating a college, one should ask the degree of success its graduates are having in locating recreation positions, and into what positions the graduates are being hired.

HIRING PRACTICES

Fortunately, the political patronage system is no longer in existence. This system allowed elected officials and political appointees to give jobs to friends and relatives, or to those who supported their campaigns. Because most, if not all, agencies which provide recreation operate under a bipartisan Civil Service Commission, with the merit system used for filling jobs and promotions, equal employment opportunity prevails. In other words, jobs are filled by examination, written and oral, and there is no discrimination because of political affiliation, or for reasons of race, religion, or sex. In recent years, an increasing number of women have shown an interest in majoring in outdoor recreation.

PERSONAL QUALIFICATIONS

Outdoor recreation is not for the person who wants to be alone in the wilderness. A candidate for this career must have a strong interest in working with and understanding people. Young people wishing to advance in this profession must have educational and experience qualifications, leadership abilities, and the maturity to conform with reasonable standards of dress and personal habits, as well as integrity and perseverance. Men and women entering this field must consider the fact that state and federal employees in park and recreation positions are usually required to move every few years. The difficulty of leaving a house, relatives, a well-loved part of the country, the spouse's job, and the children's schools and friends must not be underestimated. Duty in large cities will be inevitable for those who rise in the administrative ranks.

There also may be law enforcement duties to be carried out. Crime in outdoor recreation areas is a growing problem, and all personnel must be ready to assist in its prevention and control. Fire control and rescue work at all hours of the day or night may be required. Other useful skills include boat handling, engine maintenance, radio operation, and equipment handling. One must be punctual, industrious, and adaptable. Above all, one must be open and pleasant with all visitors, from all walks of life, many of whom will be complaining and appear to be acting "stupidly." Patience and dedication are vital. Prospective recreation specialists must ask themselves if they will be able to qualify mentally and physically to these tasks and requirements.

EMPLOYMENT OPPORTUNITIES

Specific jobs in outdoor recreation range from the seasonal entry positions of planner aids, park aids, museum aids, entrance station, and information duty persons to permanent positions of park rangers, planners, managers, interpretive specialists, naturalists, superintendents, and other similar titles. Most positions are in parks, forests, reservoirs, refuges, or comparable areas. The work centers largely around protection of both the resource and the people who use it. Entry level positions in federal agencies start at GS-5 or GS-7. Salaries in state and county positions generally parallel these levels.

Local Government

This category includes both municipal and county governments, and these, as mentioned earlier, are staffed mostly by activity-trained recreationists. The staffing of community nature centers and other interpretive positions, however, is usually by resource-oriented persons who have specialized in interpretation.

Most counties in the United States have some park system. Those which lack parks are sparsely populated, or the recreation needs are satisfied by another unit of government. Some counties have very elaborate well-funded recreation programs and require that their headquarters and field employees have some college training.

County parks are usually larger than municipal parks and, since they are located in more rural settings, are able more easily to preserve the natural environment. Employment for outdoor recreation graduates is expanding in county parks systems.

State Agencies

There is a variety of designations for state recreation lands—parks, parkways, forests, wildlife refuges, memorials, recreational areas, and historical sites. The names have different connotations in different states and may be administered by any one of a number of state agencies.

The greatest contribution to outdoor recreation by the states is through their state park systems. Visitation is mostly during the day and is heavily concentrated on weekends, causing serious overcrowding for a few hours each week. Many state parks, however, are filled to capacity all summer long. Because of their close proximity to population centers, visitation is greater than the combined use of the national parks and forests. Most state park systems require college training for their professional staffs. Advancement is generally good because the organization is large.

Other state agencies, such as state forests and refuges, also meet some of the recreation demand and employ college trained people on lands where the recreational use is heavy.

Federal Recreational Opportunities

A dozen federal agencies are directly involved in some phase of outdoor recreation. Some are in advisory capacities, but most offer recreational opportunities on the lands under their administration. The U.S. Civil Service Commission controls employment practices of federal agencies. One federal agency, the Bureau of Outdoor Recreation (BOR), administers no land but is a service agency, coordinating all federal recreation programs, and the federal-state assistance programs of the Land and Water Conservation Fund Act of 1964. BOR employees come from a variety of disciplines dealing directly as well as more remotely with outdoor recreation.

The National Park Service (NPS), in contrast to BOR, is maintained for the sole purpose of administering lands for outdoor recreation. NPS administers nearly 300 different areas, each of which has national significance. These many areas are managed under one of three categories, natural, historic, or recreation areas. The great national parks and national monuments are the best known areas; however, there are also such areas as seashores, parkways, historic sites, scenic riverways, and recreation areas. Emphasis on backgrounds for employment shifts with needs. A few years ago natural resource training was necessary. Then a social science background was preferred. Currently, training in law enforcement is favored.

The U.S. Forest Service, which administers the national forests, considers outdoor recreation one of its five major uses, along with timber, water, wildlife, and forage. The Forest Service today recognizes the recreational value of the 187,000,000 acres of lands that it administers, and attempts to integrate recreation with these other uses. Diversity of opportunities, including hunting and wilderness travel, makes its lands popular. In hiring recreation specialists, the Forest Service expects them to rise through the normal administrative channels. It requires that its employees meet Civil Service requirements for professional foresters. By selecting certain courses in four of six specialized fields of forestry, most outdoor recreation majors can easily qualify as foresters. Also, during periods of economic difficulties, when recreational employment may be down, this broader education base may be an asset.

Other agencies employing outdoor recreation graduates are the Bureau of Land Management, Army Corps of Engineers, Tennessee Valley Authority, and to a less extent the Fish and Wildlife Service and Bureau of Reclamation. Each has Civil Service requirements to be met and picks its personnel from specific federal registers. During their early college years, interested students would do well to investigate individual agency requirements.

Another opportunity, one which provides overseas experience, is working as a Peace Corps volunteer. Developing nations are in great need of qualified personnel in environmentally oriented fields, including park planners, park interpreters, and park managers. Successful candidates receive specialized training in the language and culture of the host country. A tour of duty overseas for someone just out of college can be rewarding.

Private Sector

The private sector may be broadly grouped into two categories, profit and nonprofit. The profit categories include those enterprises which charge for providing facilities and services, and also the manufacturers of recreation equipment. The nonprofit group includes lands held by industrial and agricultural owners, clubs, and conservation societies. Approximately 50 percent of all recreation usage is attributable to the private sector.

Because the private sector's role in outdoor recreation is not as well defined as is the public sector's, it is more difficult to describe job opportunities. Since there are no registers or entrance examinations, it is a matter of the individual selling himself or herself to the private organization. A well-written resume showing educational qualifications, including business courses as well as experience, is essential for obtaining employment in the private sector. A positive attitude toward the profit motive is necessary when seeking employment with commercial recreation firms.

COMPENSATION AND REWARDS

Basically, outdoor recreationists are people who are at home in the out-of-doors. Also, they enjoy caring for other people's leisure activities in the out-of-doors. The salaries and rate of advancement compare favorably with other careers in natural resources management. The rewards lie in knowing one is making a contribution to an important part of other people's lives, knowing one has completed a special kind of curriculum, and is working in a special kind of environment.

Unfortunately, when the economy declines and more people have more leisure, it causes a negative impact on employment. When people are not working, the tax base, which supports public recreation, also declines, and new jobs in outdoor recreation are scarce. At the time of this writing, however, the national economy is improving, new park establishment is going forward, and environmental awareness is still an important issue. It is to be hoped that new graduates will find ample employment opportunities in the next few years.

EDITOR'S NOTE: In this chapter, and elsewhere throughout the book, mention is made of the Bureau of Outdoor Recreation. Since the book was written, the name of the bureau has been changed to Heritage Conservation and Recreation Service.

5 Forestry

ARTHUR B. MEYER and ORLO M. JACKSON

During the last half of the nineteenth century leaders of United States public opinion began to realize that our forests could be exhausted. As a result, a few went to Europe to study in the schools of forestry, since there were none in America. Some European graduates of those schools attracted by the problems and opportunities in North America came to this country to practice their profession.

Forestry has been defined as "the scientific management of forests for the continuous production of goods and services." The key words are "continuous production." They indicate that forests produce things we need and can keep doing so without stopping. "Scientific management" is necessary to keep forests producing. "Goods" are the countless products of wood, from lumber to paper and plastics, as well as forage for livestock, and crops of wildlife. "Services" are not grown but come about because forests and forest lands exist. Probably the most important service is the beneficial effect forests have upon the nation's water supplies. Forests are places where people by the millions may enjoy outdoor recreation in its many phases. Forests also are places where scientists and others may study nature in the wild and where those who appreciate natural beauty may go for inspiration.

Professional foresters provide plans for, manage, and protect our renewable, natural forest resources. With their expert care, forests will continue to supply their bounty for human needs.

Using a paint gun, a forester marks a mature pine tree to be removed in a harvest cut. (Photo by U.S. Forest Service.)

As a field of employment, professional forestry has shown steady growth in this country during the twentieth century. In the early 1900s, all the professional foresters in the United States could hold a meeting in a medium sized office. In 1962, there were an estimated 19,000 foresters in forestry and closely allied fields. Today (1978) their numbers are estimated at 30,000.

The creation of the Forest Service in the U.S. Department of Agriculture to replace that Department's Bureau of Forestry provided the first significant employment opportunities for forestry professionals. The Forest Service was assigned the responsibility for managing the national forests. The states were not long behind the federal government in their recognition of the importance of our forest lands. Encouraged by funds for forestry available under the Weeks Law of 1911 and the Clarke-McNary Act of 1924, many states established state forestry agencies, another market for the profession. Still more employment opportunities became available as forest industry acquired land to support its mills and realized that foresters were needed to direct activities.

EDUCATIONAL REQUIREMENTS FOR THE PROFESSION

College training leading to the bachelor of science degree is required of the professional forester. Advanced scholastic work and graduate degrees are necessary in some fields of specialization and helpful in others.

Specialization in high schools is neither necessary nor desirable. The prospective forester should acquire as broad a cultural background as possible. Certain basic subjects, however, should be taken. These include chemistry and physics, biological sciences, English composition and literature, public speaking, and mathematics.

College instruction in forestry consists of a foundation of basic scientific, engineering, economic, and social studies courses, followed by technical training in five professional subject areas. The Society of American Foresters established these areas along with curriculum standards to be met by colleges and universities for accreditation. They are forest biology, forestry in social context, forest resources inventory, forest ecosystem management, and forest resources administration.

Examples of courses falling in the realm of forest biology include dendrology, forest genetics, forest physiology, and wood structure.

Forestry in social context includes courses in forest policy, forest economics, forest law, forest sociology, and public involvement.

Forest resources inventory includes instruction in biometrics, timber measurement, photogammetry, and forest valuation.

Forest ecosystem management courses expose the student to forest protection (entomology, pathology, fire science), forest utilization, forest engineering, forest management, and silviculture. For the

forester desiring a broader base in multiple use, the curriculum generally provides courses in range management, wildlife management,
and watershed management.

Examples of forest resources administration are land-use planning, decision making, and forest business administration.

Professional forestry education began in the United States in
1898 when the Biltmore Forest School was established in North Carolina. The State College of Forestry at Cornell University was established in the same year. Both schools have since been discontinued.
Yale University School of Forestry, founded in 1900, is the oldest,
continuously operating forestry school in the United States. Today
52 schools offer professional forestry education, 43 of which are
accredited by the Society of American Foresters. In addition, 49 technician schools, most of which offer 2-year programs which can lead
to an associate degree, are recognized by the Society of American
Foresters.

Accredited Schools

The Society of American Foresters maintains a Committee on Accreditation. Its purpose is periodically to assign teams to evaluate
school programs for the teaching of professional forestry. Based upon
the team's report, the Committee on Accreditation recommends to
the Council, Society of American Foresters, to accredit or withhold
accreditation of the school. The Council makes the final decision.
From these actions is compiled a list of accredited forestry schools.
The accredited institutions meet standards which warrant the admission of graduates in approved curriculums to membership in the
Society without further proof of competence. The "approved curriculums" constitute a body of instruction containing the five subject-
matter fields defined above.

The increased scope and complexity of forestry as a profession
led the Society of American Foresters to define a core curriculum, as
well as guidelines for specialization. Forestry was this country's first
recognized professional career in natural resource conservation. A
forester's training covered in varying degrees such closely allied
resource-management fields as recreation and wildlife, watershed, and
range management. Although, as a land manager, a forester must still

possess a working knowledge in these fields, each of these fields has developed a sufficient degree of specialization to have attained status in its own right. It would be erroneous to attribute to forestry the role of sole parent of these allied fields, but the basic relationships are apparent. Furthermore, training in these fields is often provided in schools other than forestry schools.

Increase in the Number of Forestry Students

The *Journal of Forestry* periodically publishes statistics from the schools of forestry. The number of undergraduate degrees granted has shown a gradual increase: one in 1900; 160 in 1920; 1,072 in 1940; 2,321 in 1950 (influx of war veterans); 1,568 in 1961; 3,067 in 1972; 4,256 in 1976.

In earlier years most foresters graduated with degrees in forest management. Following World War II, however, many schools broadened their curriculums and granted degrees that differentiated between the various curriculums. A breakdown of the undergraduate degrees granted in 1976 follows:

	Number	Percent
Forestry	2,636	62
Wildlife	678	16
Products	264	6
Recreation	315	7
Other	363	9
Total	4,256	100

Forestry now includes forest management, urban forestry, forest engineering, and general forestry. Products includes wood science, and pulp and paper technology. Recreation includes park administration. Other includes forest soils, entomology, pathology, range management, watershed management, hydrology, environmental conservation, and forest ecology.

Forestry is no longer a "for men only" profession. Of the 4,256 baccalaureate degrees awarded in 1976, 489 or over 11 percent were awarded to women. In the same year 616 master's degrees and 136 doctor's degrees were granted in these various curriculums. The largest undergraduate enrollment of forestry students in the history of American forestry education occurred in the fall of 1976. Of the total 21,757 students, 3,920 or 18 percent were women.

More highly specialized knowledge and skills are developed as the student works toward advanced degrees. Although not essential for entry into the profession, a master's degree is increasingly desirable. The master's degree is necessary in research or teaching, and the doctorate is almost essential for maximum development of a career in either.

Two schools, at Yale and Duke Universities, offer degrees only at the graduate level. Other colleges offer courses in forestry, but grant no degrees in the subject.

Scholarships and fellowships of various kinds are available from most schools of forestry. They vary from small annual amounts to substantial contributions toward an undergraduate degree or graduate training. Some are financed by endowments or by direct awards from individuals and industrial organizations. Interested persons should make direct inquiries to the schools of their choice for financial aid available to qualified students.

A STRONG CONVICTION AS TO VALUE

Success in any walk of life requires honesty, industry, reliability, and courage. The forester also needs above-average intelligence, initiative, self-reliance, the ability to work well with other people, a scientific curiosity, and a genuine liking for the out-of-doors. Perhaps above all it is necessary to have a strong conviction of the value of his or her work and an intense interest in it.

The physical requirements of the work should be neither exaggerated nor ignored. It is necessary that a forester have good health and a reasonably strong constitution. Long periods of vigorous physical activity are often required. Sometimes, such as in fire fighting, actual physical hardship is experienced. It is important to note that most female foresters have been equal to the demands. Also, while more limited, there are some opportunities for the physically handicapped.

Both the young forester and his family should be prepared to live in isolated locations or in small rural communities adjacent to forested areas and to do without many of the advantages of urban existence. Many assignments require that the forester be away from home for extended periods of time. Such assignments must be recognized as a possible cause of emotional hardship on the forester's spouse. Especially in the early years, frequent change in location is common.

As individuals progress to positions of increasing responsibility, they are usually more permanently situated and often are stationed in cities or large towns. Paradoxically, the older forester thereupon must adjust to paperwork, office hours, and traffic jams!

EMPLOYMENT

Since World War II, there has been a tremendous expansion in the practice of forestry by industrial and private owners of timberland. This expansion has brought a considerable change in the employment of foresters and greatly increased their opportunities. Before this, most foresters worked for federal and state agencies.

As mentioned earlier, there are now (1978) an estimated 30,000 professional foresters in the United States working in forestry or in fields normally requiring a forestry background. About 50 percent work for public forestry agencies—federal, state, and local. Approximately 33 percent is employed by private industry or is self-employed. Some 6 percent work as consultants or are employed by consultants. The remaining 11 percent is in teaching and research.

Unfortunately in 1977, the number of forestry graduates exceeded employment opportunities. This condition was not unique to forestry, but was a difficulty experienced by most college majors in the 1970s. The World War II baby boom, "earthday," and many other reasons have been advanced. No single cause can be identified, but two major changes in employment opportunities resulted. First, the total number of employment opportunities in forestry had fallen to about one-half the number of graduating seniors, and secondly, opportunities for the genuinely motivated graduates increased substantially and were greatly broadened. Those students with advanced degrees experienced better employment opportunities.

Since employment opportunities for foresters fluctuate, a potential forester may find it difficult to project his employment success. As in all disciplines, however, the capable and motivated graduate seldom experiences difficulty in finding employment.

The kinds of duties foresters perform vary widely. Foresters engage in administrative work, in scientific research, in teaching, and in activities of a purely business nature which utilize their technical knowledge. They fight forest fires, insects, and diseases. They survey forest and range lands, build roads, supervise the cutting of forest products and their manufacture and sale. They plant trees, run sawmills, and do public relations work. They manage land, develop multiple-use and land management plans, provide impact surveys and work with environmental protection agencies, both federal and state. Each in his way contributes to better protection and management of the forest resources of the nation.

Federal Forestry

Since it is the oldest field of employment for foresters, federal service is the one best understood by the public. The Forest Service, United States Department of Agriculture, accounts for the majority of federal positions. Foresters are also found in agencies of the Department of the Interior (Bureau of Land Management, National Park Service, Bureau of Indian Affairs, Bureau of Sport Fisheries and Wildlife), and there are a limited number in other branches of the federal government.

In order to enter the U.S. Forest Service, an application must be made to the U.S. Civil Service Commission. Based on personal work experience, college transcript, and veterans preference the CSC evaluates the application and, if satisfactory, assigns a grade. The applicant is then placed on the Forester register. In order to determine eligibility requirements an applicant should review the current Civil Service Commission announcement.

The young forester, after receiving his civil-service appointment, would probably be assigned to a ranger district (administrative unit) of one of the country's 150 plus national forests. There, under the supervision of the district ranger, he will be engaged in many activities including cruising (inventorying) timber, surveying boundary lines, controlling fires or epidemics of insects or disease, planting trees, marking (selecting) timber for sale to wood-using industries, carrying on range-forage surveys or improvements. Also, he will find himself a member of interdisciplinary teams preparing land management plans and public impact surveys. He will be concerned with supervising the work of subprofessional employees such as fire lookouts and fire fighters, and dealing with public users of the forest, campers, tourists, ranchers and farmers, timber cutters, or residents of towns and cities in or near the forest. Other beginning foresters are assigned to research work for one of the nine regional forest and range experiment stations of the Forest Service.

In the Forest Service forest administration is centered around the functions of the district ranger who administers the management and protection of a portion of a national forest. The jobs of the ranger are extremely diverse. He is the custodian and multiple-use manager of a large and highly valuable area of public property that must serve many uses in the public interest. Under the ranger are professionals, technicians, laborers, and other support personnel.

The ranger must, in turn, answer to the forest supervisor, on whose staff are a varying number of staff specialists responsible for specific fields of work on the forest. These include such activities as timber management, or the planning of harvest and sales, recreation management, wildlife management; watershed management; reforestation, fire protection; and so on.

The forest supervisor reports to the regional forester, who administers a number of national forests and oversees cooperative activities with states and private landowners.

The regional forester also has a staff of professionals, each with designated responsibilities. The regional foresters work directly under the chief of the Forest Service, who combines with his deputy chiefs and their staffs to make up the headquarters of the Forest Service in Washington, D.C.

State Service

There is considerable similarity between the work in federal and in state service, although different states have varying types of forestry agencies. One major difference is that a large part of state forestry programs is concerned with aiding and assisting private owners of timberland, although many states have extensive forests. Almost always the forest fire control organization on a statewide basis is operated by the state service, and fire control is usually a state's largest forestry activity. Other activities include protecting and managing state-owned forests, supplying forest management and marketing assistance to private owners, producing and distributing seedling trees, administrating tax or other laws relating to forestry, educational and public relations work, and participating in the development of environmental impact statements and surveys.

Most states have a merit basis for employment. The applicant may be required to pass a competitive examination or may gain entrance through personal interviews and a study of his college and past-employment records. Thirteen states presently (1978) require registration and licensing of professional foresters.

County and Municipal Forestry

Forestry job opportunities with the small units of government may include managing a forested area which is the watershed of a city's water supply. The county or municipal forester will be concerned with forest-management practices similar to those of a federal or state forest property—in a county or city forest. The forester might be primarily involved with forest-park and recreational development and administration. Municipal foresters often have duties involving a knowledge of arboriculture and shade-tree work. In recent years there has been a marked increase in forestry students taking the urban and community forestry option offered by some universities.

Education and Extension Work

Extension work is the specialized field of group forestry educational activities carried on in conjunction with the general public, usually in agricultural areas. Extension foresters are generally attached to state land grant universities. Ability in public speaking and in writing and an ability to work with people singly or in large groups are essential.

Foresters in the field of education usually teach professional subjects in a college of forestry. Some conduct courses in forestry in agricultural or other colleges, or teach general conservation in schools or colleges offering such work for the nonprofessional student.

Teachers in professional forestry schools normally engage in research work in addition to their teaching. Occasionally staff members are concerned solely with research.

Private and Industrial Employment

More foresters are now working for industrial and private owners of timberland than at any time in our history. The nature of their work covers almost every conceivable phase of technical forestry, the business aspects of growing, harvesting, and marketing the products of forests, and related duties.

The major industrial employers of foresters are the pulp and paper companies, and logging, lumbering, and milling companies. Other types of employers include merchandisers of wood products, various types of forest-products industries, a few transportation and communications companies, producers of nursery stock, and tree-expert or arboriculture companies.

Usually industrial foresters are timberland managers. They have a great deal to do with planning or supervising logging or pulpwood cutting and with producing a future supply of raw material. This is a job that uses every phase of forestry knowledge. In recent years industrial foresters have been confronted with land use planning and consideration of environmental impacts upon the land. Foresters in industry, however, may be found working in a capacity not directly related to technical forestry work. They may be found in the sales part of businesses, concerned with manufacturing processes, or engaged in public-relations work.

Only a forester's ability and the interests and scope of activity of his employer are the limiting factors in industrial employment. It is not unusual to find foresters who have advanced to positions of great responsibility in industrial organizations. A 1976 survey of 18 major forest industry companies showed that 34 percent of the vice presidents who had forestry related responsibilities had a forestry degree.

Self-employment

Of increasing significance in the field of employment for foresters is consulting work. Here, the professional forester advises and assists private landowners, either individuals or corporations, and occasionally public agencies, in forest management planning, inventories and appraisals, aerial photography and mapping, timber and land classification, feasibility and development analyses. Many also provide complete environmental services. Some consultants operate alone as individual practitioners. Others have formed corporations or firms. There are currently over 300 firms or individuals listed as consultants in this country, and it is probably the field of employment in which potential enlargement is proportionally the greatest. Many of these consultant firms operate on an international as well as national basis.

Most successful consultants enter the field after some years of experience with industry or government or employment in a consulting firm. To operate individually as a consultant requires a background of knowledge and experience. Furthermore, it is essential for the individual to have sufficient financial resources to establish a practice.

Miscellaneous and Allied Fields

The number of professionals with a forestry education employed in fields closely allied to forestry is large enough to deserve more than minor mention. These fields include wildlife and range management, soil analysis and erosion control, some types of engineering, park development and management, shade-tree and landscape work, and various occupations in industry requiring a knowledge of wood technology.

Foreign Employment

A few foresters are employed by the Agency for International Development (Department of State) on foreign-aid assignments, and a small number of American foresters are with the Food and Agriculture Organization of the United Nations. Industrial concerns with

foreign interests employ some foresters, and some consultants specialize in foreign assignments.

REWARDS AND SATISFACTIONS

In considering a career, different people place emphasis upon different
aspects of what they hope "to get out of it." Nevertheless, in any
type of work, a person is interested in: an income sufficient to support
himself and his family and a chance for advancement in relation to
his abilities; personal satisfaction in the work; a feeling that the work
is important to society; an opportunity to develop the use of abilities
to the fullest extent possible.

Income

Foresters are in the middle income bracket. Their pay is comparable
to that of other workers in the agricultural and natural sciences, but
in general lower at the start than that of physical scientists and engineers.

A survey of professional income conducted by the Society of
American Foresters has shown a narrow range of starting salaries in
the various classes of employment. They closely approximate the
civil service starting salary at which foresters enter federal employ.
After experience is gained, however, median income shows a definite
relation to type of employer, with median salaries ranked in the following decreasing order: federal government; educational institution;
private industry; consultant or self-employed; state government. The
highest salaries are achieved in private industry. The survey showed
a remarkable uniformity of income between regions of the country.

Personal Satisfaction

Forestry offers a peculiarly stimulating combination of intellectual
and physical endeavor and a clean, vigorous, healthful way of life,
mentally and physically.

It is a deep personal satisfaction to work with growing things, to have continued contact with out-of-doors and the forces of nature. As a scientist the forester is trained to observe and understand, within the limits of scientific knowledge, what he sees. This fosters an appreciation of both the interdependence of living things and the very marvel of life itself, and it is not without its influence on the way a person thinks or the values to which he or she attaches importance.

Foresters usually have considerable opportunity to travel, to work in different parts of the nation, or even the world, and they come into contact with a wide variety of people.

Among members of the profession, there is a strong sense of comradeship that is a source of continual pleasure.

Foresters know their work is of lasting public value.

All in all, forestry offers a well-rounded, diversified, and interesting type of work that is a source of great satisfaction to those who, by their aptitudes and capabilities, are suited to it.

Social Significance

The profession of forestry is primarily concerned with the wise use and conservation of one of our country's most important possessions —forests and forest lands and their related resources. Whether the forester works for a public agency, for industry, or for himself, the practice of the profession is directed toward making these resources continuously productive for the direct and indirect benefit of individuals, industries, and the general public. It is appropriate to quote the objective of the Society of Amercian Foresters:

> "The objectives of the Society shall be to advance the science, technology, education and practice of professional forestry in America and to use the knowledge and skill of the profession to benefit society."

The social significance of forestry may be read across the face of America's forest lands, in the payrolls of her mighty forest industries, in irrigation districts whose water comes from the mountain forests, in the survival of many species of her wildlife, in the tanned face of a youngster returning from summer camp, in the wood pulp of the daily newspaper. Its significance can be written in even bigger letters for the coming generations of Americans.

Opportunity for Personal Development

Forestry is a growing profession that is expanding its responsibilities in widening fields of activity in industry and government. Foresters find that their training and the diversity of the work of forestry offer almost unlimited opportunity to make use of special personal abilities and talents. It can be said without reservation that the opportunity for personal development is entirely up to the individual.

6 Freshwater Resource Management

ROBERT T. LACKEY

In 1976, nearly 28 million Americans over the age of 16 purchased fishing licenses costing a total of more than $150 million. An additional amount spent on fishing (boats, motors, tackle, camping gear, motels, food, entrance fees, and field clothing) was much greater than license sales. Many communities are dependent on tourism as their major industry, and many tourist areas are popular because of fishing opportunities.

Fisheries science is the profession concerned with this large and important industry and with the effective management of our freshwater renewable natural resources.

FISHERIES SCIENCE DEFINED

A fishery is an aquatic, renewable, natural resource composed of three interacting components: aquatic *habitat*, aquatic *biota*, and the *human use* of the aquatic biota.

Aquatic habitat is the physical component of a fishery, as lake, pond, or stream water quality, soil characteristics, and bottom shape and contour.

Fisheries biologists collecting trout with electric shocking instruments in order to weigh and measure them and to take scale samples. (Photo by U.S. Fish and Wildlife Service.)

Aquatic biota, the second component, is represented by the animals and plants in a fishery. The biotic component ranges from microscopic plankton to higher plants, and, of course, all kinds of fish.

The third component of a fishery deals with man's use of the biota, usually fish (although fishing for food or sport includes harvest of trout, crabs, catfish, frogs, shrimp, clams, oysters, bass, kelp, sponges, whales, and other forms of aquatic biota). Man's effects on aquatic biota may also be caused by industrial, agricultural, and domestic water used for waste chemical disposal, irrigation, or drinking.

When we treat the two fisheries components, aquatic habitat and aquatic biota together, we are simply looking at an *aquatic ecosystem.* Aquatic ecology—the study of the relationships between animals, plants, and their environment—is a complex field in its own right. When one adds a third component, human use, the discipline becomes even more complex—the hallmark of all areas of renewable natural resources management.

Many problems confront a fisheries scientist attempting effectively to manage a fishery. For example, suppose that a manager, employed by a state fish and wildlife agency, is responsible for managing a large reservoir, a mountain lake, or a coastal river. He routinely faces a number of problems and constraints in carrying out his assignment.

Largely Uncontrollable Nature of Aquatic Environments

Fisheries managers are often faced with the frustrating reality that they can only partially control or influence aquatic environments. The number and kinds of habitat changes possible in a reservoir, lake, or river environment are few. Certainly the gross degradation of aquatic ecosystems by pollution often can be eliminated, but excessive runoff resulting from widespread land-use practices (i.e., urban, agricultural, road construction) is much more difficult to control. While alteration of aquatic habitat for increased fish production is possible in most fisheries, it is most applicable in streams and ponds.

Natural Variation in Animal and Plant Populations

All populations undergo a certain amount of natural fluctuation. Crappie, for example, may be common in a lake during one year and rare the next. Many population variations are poorly understood and take place at unpredictable intervals.

Dynamic Aspects of Biotic Populations

All animal and plant populations under natural conditions are in a state of change even though the population may appear to be stable. The total weight of fish, or other animals or plants, may be roughly the same year after year. However, the rate of death, birth, predation, growth, or harvest may be drastically different.

Conflicting Desires Within the General Public

Lakes, reservoirs, rivers, streams, and ponds may be used by anglers, boaters, bird watchers, water skiers, farmers (irrigation), industrial interests (electrical generation, manufacturing), cities and towns (drinking water), and many other segments of society. Many of these uses cause severe conflicts. As an example, reservoir water for agricultural irrigation often precludes quality fishing opportunities because of excessive lake drawdown. No one likes to drag a boat over extensive mud flats, but fewer people yet want to pay more for food.

Conflicting Desires Within the Fishing Public

Anglers themselves rarely agree on what a fishery should produce. Should a particular resource be managed for trophy trout or "fryers," for hatchery or native trout, for "catch and release" fishing or for consumption? These are some of the real and routine conflicts that face any fisheries manager.

Inadequate Information for Management Decisions

As is true in all areas of conservation, there is rarely enough information available to make management recommendations and decisions. Often a fisheries scientist must recommend positions and policies with relatively little available ecological or sociological data. What will be the impact of channeling a stream on the aquatic ecosystem? How will this channeling affect public recreational opportunities? How does society feel about the trade-offs in such decisions?

Now that a fishery has been defined and some of the problems facing fisheries scientists have been identified, the profession of fisheries science can now be described. Fisheries science is clearly a blend of numerous disciplines, including management, biology, economics, chemistry, law, political science, sociology, psychology, mathematics, statistics, and others. All are oriented toward manipulating a fishery for its best societal use. Each of these disciplines is an important facet of fisheries science, and often all or many must be brought to bear on solving a single fisheries problem.

Management

This is the study of how to evaluate and implement decisions to meet specified goals and objectives. Most management principles are universal, but their application is highly variable. A manager in a commercial enterprise may measure his success by profit or income. The manager of a state or federal fisheries agency has a more nebulous objective or "bottom line." Certainly the fisheries manager is attempting to maximize the outdoor recreational experience through the aquatic resource, but how is this measured? Is it the number of fish in the creel, or the quality of the fishing experience, the total number of days spent fishing by the public, or the quality of the aquatic environment? Clearly the bottom line in fisheries management is often unclear.

Biology

Biology is a major contributing discipline to fisheries science. Information on the life history and physiological requirements of many animal and plant species is needed to manage fisheries. Simple questions, such as "when do fish spawn?" must be answered and answered accurately for effective fisheries management decisions. The behavior of animals must also be understood by fisheries scientists. Why are hatchery-reared trout more susceptible to predation than wild trout? What is the behavioral mechanism operating? Another example of the role of biology in fisheries management is determining the physiological mechanisms of pollution-caused deaths. If it is known what physiological changes take place in fish subjected to pollution, it may be possible to eliminate the specific toxic substances.

Economics

This discipline is increasingly becoming an important facet of fisheries science. The question of how society places a value on tangibles and intangibles affects all management-oriented professions, including those in conservation. Because trade-offs (jobs vs. environment, stocking fish vs. natural reproduction, commercial vs. recreational fishing interests) are at the base of all fisheries management decisions, the principles of economics are useful to fisheries scientists. Benefit/cost analyses are typically used to determine if "public works" projects are worthwhile by comparing the total benefits to the public against the total costs to the public. Such projects and benefit/cost analyses have far reaching impacts on America's fisheries resources.

Chemistry

The study of chemistry allows fisheries scientists to understand the chemical interaction of water and biota. Water contains many naturally occurring and human caused chemical constituents. These chemicals have a tremendous effect on aquatic biota. They permit life to exist in water and they may, under certain circumstances, limit the biotic potential of a stream, pond, or lake. Pollution through undesirable chemical addition to water is an example of an important problem for which a knowledge of chemistry has been useful to fisheries scientists.

Law

Law, especially related to environmental issues, is important to the practicing fisheries scientist. Few fisheries scientists are lawyers, but with so many conservation issues and problems being solved in courts, the fisheries scientist must be familiar with legal institutions and the relevant conservation and environmental legislation. The floor of the courtroom is often the arena where management recommendations are accepted or rejected. Increasingly, scientists and managers are being called as expert witnesses in complex conservation issues.

Political Science

Politics is a more important facet of fisheries science than many people wish to admit. Like it or not, fisheries scientists must recognize that decisions affecting fisheries resources are often societal decisions arrived at through governmental processes rather than purely scientific analysis. The political arena provides the means to resolve conflicts between uses and factions of society. How does society decide whether or not a dam will be built that causes extinction of a species? Can a dam project be abandoned causing the loss of many jobs and recreational opportunities associated with the lake?

Sociology and Psychology

These seldom used to be considered integral to fisheries science, but this view has changed dramatically. How people perceive fishing and fisheries problems and how they react to different management decisions are now important areas of fisheries science. We can often manipulate aquatic biotic or habitat components to adjust to public preferences, but molding public preferences to biotic and habitat needs is more difficult. Public education programs in conservation are often based on sociological or psychological approaches.

Mathematics

This is essential to modern fisheries science. The study of animal and plant populations is a highly quantitative endeavor. Mathematical analysis enables the scientist or manager to simplify information into general relationships. It is how we translate descriptive information into quantitative information. Mathematics may be used to describe processes (i.e., mortality rates, growth rate) and to predict the future based on current mathematical relationships (i.e., future fish yield under certain fishing regulations).

Statistical Inference

In its simplest form statistical inference permits the fisheries scientists to attach probability to their answers, conclusions, or recommendations. If a fisheries scientist wished to determine which of several new hatchery diets is best for growing rainbow trout, he would design a statistically valid trial test. Through statistical inference, he could attach a probability to the correctness of his answer.

Engineering

These studies are necessary or at least desirable in many areas of fisheries science. Interaction with engineers is necessary in modifying proposed dams, designing hatcheries or stream-improvement structures, developing sampling and field equipment, and designing experimental facilities. Fisheries scientists, knowing and appreciating what is feasible in road construction, can protect fisheries resources by insisting that designers and builders do their work a certain way. They can demand that logging roads be located in only certain areas and can literally save mountain streams from destruction.

Computer Technology

Computers, a recent addition to fisheries science, can perform easily computational tasks, but, as rapidly processed data become available to managers, more demands are placed on the individual to make rational use of this increased information. Far from replacing man, computers have made certain individuals desirable, if not indispensable, to modern society.

Many other disciplines are important in fisheries science. A key point to remember is that fisheries science is a whole collection of disciplines, not just one or two. Confronted with a particular fisheries problem, the fisheries scientist may have to draw on the collective knowledge of many diverse disciplines to solve the problem.

EDUCATIONAL QUALIFICATIONS

Fisheries scientists possess a wide variety of educational backgrounds. Formal educational backgrounds range from high school diplomas to doctorates. Laborers on hatchery, field, or construction crews need little formal education beyond high school. Professorships and high level research positions nearly always require a doctorate.

No single curriculum is universally appropriate for all areas of fisheries science, but any curriculum in fisheries science should at least include a foundation in the basic biological sciences, advanced mathematics, statistical methods, political science, sociology, psychology, computer techniques, public speaking, English composition, natural resource economics, and management concepts as applied in renewable natural resources (fisheries, forestry, and wildlife management). Students interested in population dynamics, for example, would be well advised to take additional management and mathematics courses. Students with a leaning toward fisheries policy should take additional courses in political science, law, international affairs, economics, and management. Students interested in the biological aspects of fisheries would be well advised to take additional advanced biology and chemistry courses.

The American Fisheries Society has set minimum educational requirements for certification of fisheries scientists:

	Semester Hours	Quarter Hours
Biological sciences	30	45
Physical sciences	15	22
Mathematics-statistics	6	9
Communications	6	9

At least four of the courses in biological sciences must be related to aquatic ecosystems. Mathematics should be at least at the level of college algebra, and statistics must include at least one course in statistical methods. It is important to note that these educational requirements are the minimum to meet the requirements for certification by the American Fisheries Society. Additional coursework and training beyond these minimums are highly desirable, if not necessary, to secure most fisheries positions.

Although no one knows precisely how many fisheries scientists are graduated each year in the United States and Canada, the number is approximately 1000 at the bachelor's level, 300 at the master's level, and 85 at the doctoral level. Many additional students are graduated in related disciplines such as wildlife, aquatic biology, natural resource economics, forestry, and outdoor recreation.

Several dozen universities offer degrees in fisheries science (see Appendix A). Others offer degrees in closely related disciplines. Some universities only offer graduate degrees in fisheries science while some community colleges only offer associate (two-year) degrees. The American Fisheries Society does not currently accredit university programs in fisheries science. The prospective student should carefully investigate various alternative programs and universities. A review of the current status of recent graduates will provide an idea of the kinds of positions likely to be available to graduates of that program.

Graduate work, including a thesis based on original research conducted by the student, is necessary for most higher level fisheries positions. Stipends in the form of teaching or research assistantships are often available to highly qualified bachelor's or master's degree graduates. Master's degrees typically require approximately two years for completion. Doctoral degrees usually require approximately three years beyond the master's.

Specialization is common in fisheries science as in most professions. While the "generalist" and fisheries manager must feel at home with biology, economics, chemistry, physics, political science, psychology, and many other disciplines, the specialist becomes an expert in one or a few facets of fisheries science. Fish parasitology is an example of a specialty. The necessary education and training in fish parasitology are extensive and concentrated in the biological area. Other common specialties are limnology, fisheries economics, population dynamics, computer applications, environmental analysis, and aquaculture. Appendix B includes references giving further details on specialties in fisheries science.

PERSONAL QUALIFICATIONS

There is no single set of personal qualifications required to be successful as a fisheries scientist. Some kinds of field work may require great physical strength and stamina. On the other hand, fisheries scientists dealing with legal issues have less need for physical attributes but must have a much greater tolerance for frustration. Desire, ambition, and intellectual ability are difficult personal characteristics to separate, but they are all important attributes of the successful fisheries scientist. The ability to persevere when confronted with complex and frustrating problems can often spell the difference between success and failure. The ability to work with people, whether they are anglers, farmers, elected officials, or other professionals, cannot be overemphasized.

The student considering a career in fisheries science should be aware that love of the outdoors, a concern for the environment, and a desire to work away from human development are poor reasons to select a career in conservation. The level of training required for professional fisheries jobs is extensive and rigorous.

There is no "typical" work in fisheries science. *Field* work may include routine hatchery operations such as fish feeding and artificial spawning, lake and stream surveys for fish population assessments, survey of fishkills and their causes, water quality determinations, chemical treatment of lakes to eliminate or reduce undesirable fish populations, life history studies, fish population analysis, aquatic herbicide treatment, creel surveys, angler surveys, and many other types of varied and important activities.

Laboratory Work

Chemical analyses, physiological determinations, diet and nutrition studies, and behavioral studies are a few examples. Evaluation of data by statistical analysis and report writing are a large part of both laboratory and field work.

Analytical Evaluation

Often fisheries problems can and should be solved without collecting additional data. Perhaps we may already know enough about a fish population to develop harvest regulations if we carefully analyze existing data mathematically. Many of the underlying principles upon which we base management were developed or crystallized by analysis of existing data.

Interaction

Work with other professionals in other agencies, special interest groups, and the general public is a more common type of fisheries work than most people realize. Many fisheries scientists spend their entire careers representing their agency's interests in interagency dealings and negotiations. Often such interaction is the most effective way to protect the environment from unnecessarily damaging "development." Interaction with special interest groups such as sportsmen clubs, environmental groups, and hiking clubs may be crucial in gaining support for a particular management program. Effective interaction with the general public is also important in fisheries science.

Teaching

In fisheries science this is mostly limited to the university level. There has been a slow but steady expansion in the numbers of professorships in fisheries science, but the total number is not large. Professors are usually involved in ongoing research projects in addition to their teaching duties.

The American Fisheries Society has promulgated a "Code of Practices" for members. The code specifies professional standards in relations with the general public, the quality and type of professional services provided, relations with clients and employers, and relationships with other professionals. Copies of the code can be obtained from the American Fisheries Society, 5410 Grosvenor Lane, Bethesda, Md., 20014.

EMPLOYMENT OPPORTUNITIES

Fisheries science is a relatively small profession. There are only about 10,000 fisheries scientists in North America (bachelor's degree or higher). The number is slowly and steadily increasing. Employment opportunities vary greatly among the disciplines of fisheries science, at different educational and experience levels, and in different geographic regions.

Summer positions are helpful in gaining experience and in increasing chances of locating a permanent job after completion of a university education. Many summer and permanent positions deal with fisheries problems but may be called something else: aquatic scientist, wildlife biologist, research scientist, environmental scientist, biologist, and others.

Federal Government

The Fish and Wildlife Service, National Marine Fisheries Service, Forest Service, Bureau of Land Management, and Environmental Protection Agency are the largest federal employers of fisheries scientists. Other federal agencies such as the Nuclear Regulatory Commission, Tennessee Valley Authority, Bureau of Reclamation, Army Corps of Engineers, and Soil Conservation Service also employ fisheries scientists.

State Government

State fish and wildlife agencies have historically been the principal employer of fisheries scientists. Recently, state environmental protection agencies have been hiring a substantial number of fisheries scientists. Most of the traditional fisheries management activities are carried out by state agencies.

Local Government

Employment opportunities in fisheries science with county, city, or town governments are limited. Many local governments do employ professionals to manage parks and wildland resources, but employment of fisheries scientists is generally left to the state government.

International Government

The United Nations Food and Agriculture Organization and the U.S. Agency for International Development are the main employers of fisheries scientists for fisheries problems abroad. Most international jobs for freshwater fisheries scientists relate to aquaculture and pond management in developing countries. Production of fish for food is the main thrust of international activities in fisheries science.

Universities and Colleges

Opportunities for fisheries scientists in academia are limited. Professorships and most permanent university research positions require a doctorate. Students aspiring to become professors should obtain a broad background (preferably both geographic and academic) while pursuing their bachelor's, master's, and doctoral degrees. Academic openings for technicians and research assistants are limited.

Utilities

There has been a dramatic increase in job opportunities for fisheries scientists with utility companies. Public awareness and legislation have resulted in hiring professionals by utility companies to provide inhouse knowledge to minimize environmental damage caused by electrical power generation, dam and transmission line construction and maintenance, and other activities.

Industry

Environmental awareness in the 1960s and 1970s has resulted in a much greater employment demand for all kinds of environmental scientists. Fisheries scientists are often the ideal individuals for these jobs, although few are explicitly identified as fisheries positions. Determining the toxicity of chemicals is a major activity of many of these positions.

Engineering Firms

Project design for dams, electrical generating plants, irrigation systems, and water diversion used to be solely concerned with engineering requirements. Environmental factors now must be considered throughout the project's design process. Fisheries scientists can often perform a valuable role when employed by engineering firms.

Consulting

An increasing number of fisheries scientists are able to work full time through private consulting to help solve fisheries problems confronting public and private organizations. Most professors are also part-time consultants. Consulting problems often relate to environmental issues and how to minimize damage to the aquatic environment.

The organizations listed in Appendix C provide further information on employment opportunities in fisheries science.

COMPENSATION AND REWARDS

Salaries in fisheries science in general are not commensurate with the training required. Average salaries are lower than medicine, law, dentistry, or engineering with comparable education and training. Salaries within the profession typically follow civil service scales. While there is little opportunity to become rich through employment as a fisheries scientist, an adequate income can be realized.

Beyond the monetary rewards, there is the opportunity to protect and use wisely for society aquatic renewable natural resources. This opportunity may well be the greatest reward for any of the conservation professions.

7 Marine and Estuarine Resource Management

ERIC D. PRINCE and ROBERT T. LACKEY

Worldwide demand for fish as food for man and domestic animals, as raw material for industrial processes, and as the target of recreation is growing rapidly. For example, use of fish in Western Europe and North America has increased more than 50 percent since the late 1950s, an increase that demonstrates the expanding importance of the oceans and their estuaries as current and potential sources of protein. Increased use of fish has brought about a need for managing these resources to conserve our present reserves and insure adequate supplies for the future. Marine and estuarine resources management is the scientific profession which addresses the problems of using fisheries resources for the good of society based upon biological, economic, and sociological principles. This chapter provides a broad view of marine and estuarine resource management for those who may seek careers in this field.

The term fish means all the consumable, renewable living natural resources of the oceans and estuaries, including finfish, molluscs,

Lowering an electronically operated instrument that measures salinity, temperature, and depth, and takes water samples to determine the ocean's fertility. (Photo by National Marine Fisheries Service.)

crustaceans, marine worms, sea urchins, marine mammals and reptiles, and seaweeds.

Fisheries resources can be divided into three main categories, according to the areas in which they are found: *estuaries* at the mouths of streams and rivers; *coastal waters* over continental shelves, and *offshore waters* above continental slopes and deep ocean basins.

An estuary refers to a semienclosed coastal body of water with a free connection to the opean ocean, where the saline waters are measurably diluted by freshwater drainage from land (i.e., a stream or river emptying into the ocean). Estuarine ecosystems are characteristically inhabited by unique plant and animal populations that have adapted to the special seasonal and nutrient cycles of this environment. Because an estuary has both marine and freshwater characteristics, it overlaps freshwater resources (see chapter on Freshwater Resource Management), but is arbitrarily included in this chapter.

Coastal waters are the shallow, near shore areas over continental shelves. A continental shelf is the ocean floor formed by underwater extensions of the continents, starting from land and extending oceanward to a depth of 200 meters.

Offshore waters are the deep, mid-ocean areas above the continental slopes and deep ocean basins. Continental slopes (200 to 3000 meters deep) are sea floors that extend beyond the continental shelves at an average inclination of about 4 degrees to the deep ocean basins (3000 to 6000 meters deep). Continental slopes support the largest portion (73 percent) of the earth's water cover.

Most of the marine fish harvest (by weight) is from coastal and offshore waters. The catch from offshore waters consists primarily of finfish and is taken mainly by commercial fishing. Offshore resources are typically harvested with open water fishing gear. Many nations participate in the fisheries and many are regulated by international treaties.

Recreational fishing in the United States and Canada often plays a more important role than commercial fishing in coastal and estuarine harvests and includes more crustaceans and molluscs. Estuaries are also important spawning and nursery areas for many coastal and some offshore fishes. Coastal and estuarine waters usually come under the sovereignty of individual nations, and methods of fishery harvests in these areas consist primarily of inshore fishing fleets.

HISTORY OF THE PROFESSION

Use of marine and estuarine resources dates back thousands of years to man's initial habitation of coastal areas. Oriental and Egyptian cultures heavily exploited ocean resources by about 200 B.C. Fish populations in the Mediterranean Sea were harvested by numerous other nations by about 1000 B.C. Further use of marine resources was evident when European fisheries became prominent about 950 A.D. in the North Sea. The Newfoundland fisheries were developed in the early 1500s.

Marine finfish were the first natural resource to be used on a large scale in America, and fishing was one of our first industries. The first conservation measure in North America was adopted by the pilgrims in the early 1600s when they restricted the use of striped bass for making fertilizer. There was little management of marine resources before the 1800s, however, and harvest was essentially unregulated.

The idea that marine and estuarine resources could be overharvested and might need management arose during the 19th century and precipitated much interest. The modern scientific roots of marine and estuarine resource management might be traced back to the oceanic expeditions of the research vessel *Challenger* in 1873. These expeditions were the first major step toward understanding the oceans. Several resource conservation organizations were created in the United States during the later part of the 19th century. The American Fisheries Society, established in 1870, became the first professional natural resource society of North America. In 1872, the U.S. Fish Commission was formed and instituted fish propagation as its main policy.

During the early 1900s, marine fishing fleets were characterized by rapid expansion and advances in gear technology. The beginning of the 20th century was also marked by the general acknowledgment that some ocean resources had been depleted. Several fisheries commissions and treaties, such as the International Halibut Commission, the International Pacific Salmon Fisheries Commission, and the Bering Sea Fur Seal Treaty were established during this period, primarily to regulate the fisheries. A few, such as the International Council for the Exploration of the Sea, formed in 1902, dealt only with research.

The American Fisheries Society adopted *Maximum Sustainable Yield* as the first North American fisheries policy in 1938. Simply stated, this policy encouraged biological management of fish populations to provide the maximum sustainable number or weight of fish indefinitely into the future. Implementation of the policy in the 1940s and 1950s revealed that nonbiological factors, such as economics, politics, and social issues, also needed to be considered. One of the most important of these nonbiological factors was that of allocating property or fishing rights for marine fishes, which are a common property natural resource (i.e., a resource which belongs to no single individual or group, but to society as a whole). One of the first efforts at designating these property rights, and thus assuming the cost of using the resources, occurred at the United Nations Law of the Sea Conference in 1958. Satisfactory solutions to the property rights issue have been slow in developing, and serious conflicts still persist.

During the late 1960s and early 1970s, the maximum sustained yield policy underwent conceptual changes and evolved into the policy now being widely endorsed, *Optimum Sustainable Yield*. Theoretically, optimum sustained yield takes into account those factors that maximum sustained yield ignore, such as economical, political, and social considerations of the resource as well as biological factors. With growing concern about the adequacy of U.S. fisheries policy, Congress passed several laws in an attempt to legislate mandatory consideration of certain factors. Two of the most important acts are the Coastal Zone Management Act (1972), which attempts to protect our coastal shorelines from overdevelopment, and the Fishery Conservation and Management Act of 1976, which expanded U.S. territorial fisheries jurisdiction from a 12-mile limit to a 200-mile limit, and legally instituted the policy of optimum sustained yield.

THE PROFESSION DEFINED

Marine and estuarine fishes are harvested by commercial and recreational fishing. Although relative use varies from nation to nation, the monetary value of commercial catches worldwide almost always exceeds that of sport catches. In some areas, such as the United States, however, the expenditures related to recreational fishing are at least as high in total value as is the commercial catch. In the past, conflicts between these primary types of fishing have been evident. Use of nonliving marine natural resources (i.e., oil, coastal development, areas for military uses) has also become progressively more important in the management of commercial and recreational fishes since the demand for both types of resources (living and nonliving) has increased.

Management of any natural resource system can be defined as the judicious use of available methodology to accomplish a desired goal. This goal is generally considered the best possible use of the resource, but often varies according to what is being managed and the patterns of use.

Management goals, such as "best possible use of the resource," often resist explicit definitions because they are vague and complicated. As an example, the best possible use of a fishery may call for maximizing commercial catch, profit, or recreational use on a sustained basis, as well as simultaneously protecting the resource and environment from overuse. Since some of these goals may conflict with each other, problems arise in their practical application. In addition, managing marine and estuarine resources is difficult because of the vast size of the oceans, the high commercial value of the resources, and the complications that result because these resources overlap many international boundaries.

Nevertheless, the following general tactics and alternatives are now being applied to management of the oceans and estuaries: control and regulation of harvest and other factors affecting mortality within fish populations; providing, improving, and protecting the habitat from pollution and degradation; propagation and culture of fish to replace or supplement native populations; manipulation of the resource socially, economically, and politically for man's benefit.

Because of the complexity of marine and estuarine resource management, most management plans consist of a combination of these management tactics.

Marine and estuarine fisheries are composed of three basic interacting components: marine and estuarine *habitat* (abiotic component); marine and estuarine *organisms* (biotic component); and *man's use* of these abiotic and biotic components. Because the interactions of the major ecosystem components play a vital role in the way a system will react to various management practices, management of the whole aquatic ecosystem, rather than individual segments of a fishery, is often necessary. Therefore, understanding the principles that govern the overall system is necessary for effective natural resource management. This approach to management requires that managers have considerable formal education as a background for contributing to decision-making.

EDUCATION FOR THE PROFESSION

The level of education necessary for careers in marine and estuarine resource management often depends on the type of work desired. Guidance publications on marine and estuarine-related career opportunities describing the kinds of work available are listed in Appendix B. Resource management jobs can generally be grouped according to the type of work involved: technical work; analytical work; administration; extension; consulting; teaching, and research.

Technical level jobs involving routine field or laboratory activities, such as assisting hatchery operations, water quality determinations, or chemical analysis, usually require a bachelor's degree, or sometimes only a high school diploma. Most positions consisting of analytical work, administration, extension, consulting, teaching, or research require at least a master's degree.

Analytical work involves the mathematical analysis and interpretation of fisheries phenomena, and administration consists mostly of overseeing and directing management programs. Fisheries or marine extension agents disseminate and clarify resource management information. Both administration and extension positions often require applicants with Ph.D. degrees and the background for analytical work usually necessitates considerable graduate-level education. Teaching positions are basically restricted to the university level, but research can involve all of the work listed above. Although it is not always restricted to universities, research, as well as teaching, often requires that the candidate have a Ph.D. degree. Consulting problems are typically related to environmental issues and the development of means for reducing damage to the aquatic environment.

Thus, graduate training is often required for the more advanced careers in marine and estuarine resource management, and serious students with ability should include graduate school in their educational plans. Experience and training during the undergraduate years should be directed toward requirements for graduate admission if a higher level position is desired. On-the-job training, however, still remains an important part of the preparation for marine and estuarine resource managers.

Prospective students in marine and estuarine resource management often are confused when they are attempting to choose an appropriate college or university. Course requirements depend to a large extent on the type of curricula offered at the particular university. Basic courses usually offered in a marine and estuarine resource curriculum include: life sciences; physical and chemical sciences; social sciences, such as psychology and sociology; mathematics; statistics; humanities, including English, technical writing, and public speaking, and economics. The number of courses offered and required within these general areas also varies with the individual college or university.

About 200 colleges and universities teach courses in marine and estuarine resource management. Rapid expansions of curriculums, especially at the undergraduate level, make listing all programs difficult. Accordingly, Appendix A lists only the colleges and universities offering major marine science graduate programs. This list is intended as a general guide rather than an all-inclusive list. Schools offering programs in freshwater resource management (see chapter on Freshwater Resource Management) should not be overlooked, because many of the management principles can be applied to any aquatic environment.

Graduate schools generally require a student to have academic standing in the upper 25 percent of his graduating class, three recommendations, and high scores on verbal, quantitative, and biological Graduate Record Examinations. Skill in writing and public speaking and practical experience can also have a significant influence on admittance to graduate school, especially for those who have less than exemplary academic records.

PERSONAL QUALIFICATIONS

In assessing personal attitudes, prospective employers often look for good academic ability in combination with such factors as enthusiasm, dedication, ambition, ability to work with others, and common sense. These factors are often intangible and are particularly difficult to evaluate. A strong sense of enthusiasm and dedication can often overcome deficiencies in other qualifications. Personal recommendations are probably the most important barometer of personal attitudes and usually play a decisive role in acquiring a job or gaining admission to a graduate school.

Good physical condition is often a prerequisite for positions requiring extensive field work, such as making field collections, participating in extended cruises, and SCUBA diving. The work is sometimes so strenuous that high physical standards must be met. Most positions, however, such as those in management, administration, and research, do not require unusual physical condition or skills.

EMPLOYMENT

Employment opportunities in marine and estuarine resource management depend on the type of work desired and level of education, as well as the general economic condition of the country. State, federal, and local governments offer all the kinds of work discussed in the previous section, except for teaching. International governmental organizations, such as the Food and Agriculture Organization of the United Nations (FAO) and the Agency for International Development (AID) also afford similar opportunities for general marine work. Careers at universities are basically restricted to teaching, research, and extension. Employment with utilities (power companies), manufacturing industries, and engineering and consulting firms involves administration, some research and analytical work, and extension-type public relations.

Requirements for most jobs in the field of marine and estuarine resource management are being raised as the number of people qualified for positions increases beyond the number of jobs available. It was possible to qualify for a marine research position with a bachelor's degree 10 to 15 years ago, but now a master's degree is often the minimum requirement.

The American Fisheries Society does not now accredit fisheries programs but does certify qualified individuals as fisheries scientists. Minimum certification standards include specified minimum education backgrounds (at least to the bachelor's level) and certain specific course requirements (see Chapter on Freshwater Resource Management). Relevant professional experience is also required for certification. The American Institute of Fishery Research Biologists elects qualified individuals to membership as fisheries research biologists. Its standards are similar to those of the American Fisheries Society, but specific professional experience and accomplishments in research are stressed.

The number of active workers in marine and estuarine resource management is difficult to estimate because of the diversity of the work force. In the United States, the number certainly exceeds 10,000. It may be several times this number worldwide.

In assessing job opportunities in marine and estuarine-related careers, compared with certain other fields in natural resources, one can now be cautiously optimistic. Recent legislation dealing with coastal zone management and management of marine fisheries should increase the number of jobs in private industry, as well as in some state and federal agencies. The outlook for the future is uncertain, however, due in part to the dependence of marine resource budgetary allocations of state and federal agencies on the current economic trends in the country. Although some jobs can be expected to become available, the number may be limited.

COMPENSATION AND REWARDS

The financial rewards of careers in marine and estuarine resource management generally follow standards set by civil service agencies and vary depending on workers' education, experience, and geographical location. In recent years, the status of marine and estuarine resource managers has been popularized in the United States by television. Some of these television presentations have portrayed the profession in a glamorous light. It would be an injustice not to note that most of the activities of marine and estuarine resource managers (like all people engaged in scientific professions) are not glamorous, but often consist largely of data collection, analysis, and office work. Careers in marine and estuarine resource management can provide significant personal gratification and offer an opportunity to work outdoors, at least part of the time, in a fascinating field that promises to be of increasing importance in the future.

8 Range Management

ROBERT M. HYDE

There are many types of rangeland. Among the most common are natural grassland, shrub communities, forests, savannas, tundra, wetlands, alpine communities, and most deserts. Native vegetation common to these lands are grasses, broad-leafed plants, and shrubs.

Most forest lands support an understory of vegetation suitable for grazing by livestock and wildlife—the important users of range plants. But whether we speak of range or rangeland, the important thing to remember is that we are talking about land. Thus, range is a biological system involving all the complex interrelationships of its living and nonliving components. A basic characteristic of all rangelands is that they are most amenable to use and management to ecological principles.

Range is the world's largest land type. The earth's total land surface is composed of approximately 17 percent alpine mountain areas, barren deserts, and those lands covered by permanent snow or glaciers. Another 25 percent is forest land. Ten percent is cultivated, and about 3 percent is utilized as urban-suburban development. This then leaves about 45 percent of the world's land area in the broad category of rangeland. The overwhelming quantity of rangeland makes it important to man's welfare.

Consider the importance of some of its products and uses, including its effect on rural families and communities that depend on

Range scientists field sampling vegetation and recording the data for a management plan. (Photo by U.S. Forest Service.)

livestock grazing for their livelihood and economic stability. The consumer desires a reasonably priced diet including red meat products. The tourist seeks scenery or open space. The recreationist searches for an enjoyable outdoor experience, a healthy, viable wildlife population for aesthetics and hunting. The urban resident demands a dependable, high quality water supply. Fortunately, under proper development and management these multiple-use demands may be compatible. These and other important contributions from such a vast land area make it imperative that range be properly used and managed by professionally trained range scientists.

Today many rangelands are producing no more than half their potential. Former civilizations, great and small, have disappeared because of improper use of land and its vegetation—mistakes that the world cannot afford today. Range scientists face a dual challenge, conquering problems inherited from the past, and planning and directing both present and future range use in order to obtain the optimum benefits for mankind.

Although the range resource has been important to man since

the first hunter, range science (the organized body of knowledge that underlies the practice of range management) has emerged as a unique discipline only in the past few decades. Range science is based on ecological principles that explain the functions of biological systems and the basic knowledge of why plant communities are where they are. Ranchers and range specialists must understand the interactions among components of the range ecosystem and how they are to be managed for man's benefit. Ideally, proper range management results in a sustained yield of the products a manager desires without substantial inputs of fossil fuel and materials from outside sources.

Often range scientists manipulate some uses in such a way that other uses or values are enhanced. For instance, livestock grazing during certain times of the year may favor growth of plants needed by wildlife during critical seasons. Livestock on the rangelands are considered to have high aesthetic value to many tourists who live and work in urban areas.

The range scientist is trained to manage lands that produce herbage for all grazing animals, for aesthetic values and for watershed enhancement.

He knows about the structural components of the ecosystem and the classification of ecological units, the characterization of soil-plant relations and the interactions of plants, soils, and animals with climatic conditions.

The range scientist also possesses an understanding of the functions of the ecosystem's nutrient cycling and energy flow from one feeding level to the next, and with animal requirements for food and shelter. He is trained to predict soil-plant responses in the assessment of rehabilitation potential following drastic disturbances and to develop procedures for land reclamation and management.

Rangelands contribute more than $3 billion to the economy of 17 western states of which almost $2 billion are contributed to the 11 "public land" states. The range livestock industry is one of the employers in the region and contributes greatly to the rural economy and culture of the West.

The range scientists often work closely with other specialists in wildlife, hydrology, forestry, agronomy, recreation, and other disciplines. Similarly, they may serve as staff specialists for other ecosystem managers. It is important to recognize that range management is always much more than just working in the out-of-doors. Administrative planning, report writing, working with people, and public relations are very much a part of the range scientist's job.

EDUCATION FOR THE PROFESSION

The involvement of many skills in the management of rangelands creates special requirements. The student must, first of all, be educated in basic sciences. To this must be added knowledge of the related natural resources. Top positions go to those who not only possess depth in range science, but who also are able and willing to obtain special knowledge in areas such as range ecology, range-forest management, range conservation, range management, land resource appraisals, and range biology.

Although the range science curriculum will vary somewhat from one school to another, the normal course of study requires a thorough foundation in biology, mathematics, statistics, chemistry, and English communications. From this base, one normally proceeds to more specialized courses, such as plant taxonomy, plant physiology, plant and animal ecology, animal nutrition, soils, and geology. At the upper class level the course of study deals more specifically with range science and range management as such, concentrating on the interrelationships of:

1. Plant life, the basic product of rangeland.
2. Animal populations and their needs for food and habitat.
3. The land, the base of the range ecosystem.
4. Climatic influences.

The basic requirement for most range scientist positions is a bachelor of science degree in range science, range management, or range ecology. Advanced degrees are essential for research and teaching and are often necessary for advancement in other employment situations.

The range science curriculum may be supplemented along various lines, but it is most desirable to include elective courses in economics, other social sciences, and in related natural resource disciplines—forestry, wildlife, fisheries, and recreation.

Incidentally, summer employment is a phase of range management and is often available to qualified college students. This gives students the opportunity to earn while learning.

Perhaps a high school student is interested in the wise use and development of rangeland, that he is willing to accept the challenge, and that he likes the outdoors, gets along well with people, is observant and inquisitive, and wants to be useful. What next?

He should take the initiative and interview a professional in the area of his interest. Following this, he should contact an office of the Soil Conservation Service, Forest Service, Bureau of Land Management, County Extension Service, or visit a university having a Department of Range Science.

If it is not feasible, he should write to the Society for Range Management to seek counselling in a career in range science.

To prepare in high school for college training and a future profession in rangeland resources work, it is suggested that students:

1. Take courses in biology, mathematics, and chemistry and acquire communication skills by emphasizing English and speech.
2. Practice those skills by writing for the school paper and speaking before groups.
3. Learn to work with people by participating on school committees and engaging in social activities.

The need for specific instruction in the management of range resources has long been recognized and many schools now offer courses or degrees in this field.

Thirty-seven of these schools in Canada, the United States, and Mexico have joined together to form the Range Science Education Council (see Appendix A).

One must contact any of these schools for additional information concerning a professional career in range science or range management, its specific curriculum, and admission requirements.

Between 225 and 275 bachelor of science degrees in range management are conferred annually with 70 to 80 master of science degrees and 25 to 30 doctorates.

Scholarships and assistantships, especially at the graduate level, are available at nearly all the schools teaching range management. Individual schools should be contacted regarding scholarship or assistantship availability. Educational opportunities and career brochures are available from many of the colleges and universities (see Appendix A).

PERSONAL QUALIFICATIONS

No outstanding physical ability is required of a range scientist and a few physically handicapped people find employment. Some range scientists, however, spend considerable time alone gathering field data, and some work at high altitudes, either backpacking or riding horseback. Many range scientists are required to walk considerable distances over rough terrain in their work.

Range workers need the ability to work with people to handle delicate situations.

Most range science positions are classified as outdoor assignments that will involve working in mountainous range areas, the deserts, or the grassland plains of the western states, and some work in the range and pasture lands of the southeastern U.S.

Range scientists may take inventories of rangeland resources, including the kinds and numbers of plants and animals, and the condition of their habitat with respect to natural potential. They may develop land management plans with other specialists as an integrated approach to wise and sustained use of our rangeland resources. Recent graduates in range science are employed primarily by the U.S. Forest Service, Bureau of Land Management, and Soil Conservation Service. Private business employs range science graduates as real estate appraisers, consultants for land reclamation projects, ranch managers, and numerous other related positions.

EMPLOYMENT

The range management profession offers an opportunity to work continuously with natural resources, the improvement of environmental quality, and the basic problem of ecology.

It is estimated that between 8,000 and 10,000 trained range scientists are presently employed in the United States. Because of a wide variation in agency and institution job titles, not all are specifically labeled as "range scientists." Nevertheless, because of the growing interest in all aspects of the environment, it has been projected that the need for range scientists will increase by 33 percent in the next decade. This increase does not include the normal attrition occurring each year.

Most range scientists have been employed by federal government agencies, primarily in the Department of Agriculture (Forest Service, Soil Conservation Service, Agricultural Research Service) and the Department of Interior (Bureau of Land Management, Bureau of Indian Affairs, Bureau of Sport Fisheries and Wildlife, and Geological Survey). Although the federal government will continue as an important employer, there are many other opportunities for the range scientist.

More and more positions for range scientists are developing in private industry, such as ranch managers, research, sales, and service representatives for commercial firms, surface mine rehabilitation specialists, and as consultants or advisors with banks, insurance companies, real estate, and land management firms.

State governments employ range scientists in game and fish departments and state land agencies.

Colleges and universities employ range scientists in teaching, research, and extension positions.

Range scientists with a B.S. degree and little or no experience with the federal government, can expect to receive a GS-5 or GS-7 Civil Service rating. Those with M.S. degrees could expect a GS-7 or GS-9 rating. Those with Doctorates could receive a GS-9 or GS-11 rating. Graduates with experience may receive a higher GS rating. University faculty, state government employees, and those employed by private industry will vary widely in salary, but average salaries should be comparable to salaries in the federal government.

Due to a rapidly growing worldwide awareness of the importance of the rangeland resource, there has been a substantial increase in the demand for range scientists for foreign assignments. Positions are available with such overseas agencies as the United Nations Food and Agriculture Organization, the Agency for International Development, and the Peace Corps. There are, as well, some opportunities for direct employment by foreign governments.

Range management is open to both men and women. Much more important than gender is the individual's capabilities and desire to contribute in a meaningful way to man's welfare. The unique natural science background of the trained range specialist, plus the broad scope of experience generally provided in basic range management positions, make the range manager particularly well suited for advanced positions in government, industry, and the academic community. Government agency heads, college presidents and deans, corporate officers in the business world, and private entrepreneurs have come from the ranks of range managers.

9 Watershed Management

WILLIAM E. SOPPER and DAVID R. DeWALLE

Water is undoubtedly our most important resource, since without it all life would perish. It has been often quoted as "our most important servant and one of our greatest enemies." It has the peculiar quality of being an inexhaustible natural resource, but the total supply is constant. It is continually in motion, circulating between the atmosphere and the land through the hydrologic cycle. Although this cycle powered by the sun's energy cannot be stopped, man's use of water and activities often modify and interfere with the cycle and alter water quantity and quality. The total supply of water is probably more than adequate to meet all human needs, but the amount of water in usable quantities and qualities, available in a specific area at a specific time, is not inexhaustible.

The first colonists and early pioneers encountered an untouched wilderness—a vast land of mountains and valleys clothed in virgin forests and transected by a network of clean streams and rivers. Few problems of floods, water supply, or pollution existed. Forgetting a history of land abuse that was the demise of several early civilizations, these early settlers set out to repeat every mistake man has made since he first tilled the soil.

In his need to clear the land, much of the virgin hardwood forest

A hydrologist measuring the velocity of a small stream on a forested water-shed. (Photo by U.S. Forest Service.)

of eastern United States disappeared. Moving westward, the pioneer cleared great areas of natural forests, converting them to pasture and cropland. Continuous planting of corn soon led to soil exhaustion and erosion. Similarly, waves of settlers went through the South, clearing and burning the forests to plant corn, tobacco, and cotton. These crops provided little protection for the newly exposed soil, and, as a result, soil was lost through erosion or impoverished through the loss of fertility.

Continuing westward to escape the increasing pressure of civilization, pioneers found a tremendous expanse of plains and mountains.

Their rich and productive soils were plowed and planted to wheat. Over several decades drought and wind created a dust bowl and millions of acres of topsoil were blown away. Farther West, the pioneers found the Rocky Mountains and the Sierra Nevada and Cascade Mountains in a virgin forest condition with well-controlled streams and vegetated slopes. However, as a result of subsequent timber cutting, excessive grazing of rangeland and poor management of game populations, these virgin conditions deteriorated, and, as a direct consequence, many western watersheds are still in a fragile, unstable state.

During the past three centuries our country has grown from a small group of settlements on the East Coast to a continent-wide civilization of tremendous wealth and resources. However, this development has taken a severe toll on our water resources.

While the public was slow to realize that our water resource was being exploited in the name of progress, a few individuals with foresight raised their voices. One of these was George Perkins Marsh, who, in 1864, wrote a book called *Man and Nature*. In it he stressed the vital function of forests as watersheds in relation to floods and erosion. It was evident to him that forested watersheds were nature's own conservers of water and soil. He was aware that current knowledge was insufficient, and he pleaded for a research program that might develop the needed technology to protect and manage our forests and water resource.

His pleas fell mostly on deaf ears. The first federal action came over 30 years later with the passage of the Federal Reserve Act of 1897. This Act provided for the protection and improvement of forests in the headwaters of navigable rivers. Watershed research was initiated in 1909 by the U.S. Forest Service. These early efforts were meager and an expanded research effort in watershed management, forest influences, and soil and water conservation was not inaugurated until the 1930s by the Forest Service and the Soil Conservation Service. These activities were further enhanced by the enactment of the Omnibus Flood Control Act of 1936 and the Watershed Protection and Flood Prevention Act of 1954.

Growing public awareness about watershed management was probably best manifested in the Multiple Use Act of 1960 pertaining to the management of national forests. The Act directs that these lands should be managed for the production and use of all their goods and services, which include wood, water, forest, wildlife, and recreation.

The most recent national policies relating to watershed management have focused on water pollution. Legislation such as the National Environmental Policy Act of 1971 requires an assessment of the environmental impact of major construction projects. The Federal Water Pollution Control Act of 1972 necessitates specifications for best management practices to control non-point source water pollution, and the Safe Drinking Water Act of 1974 establishes strict monitoring and water quality limits for drinking water. These have all had a major impact on the responsibilities of the watershed manager. This legislation has been derived from an unprecedented general public ecological awareness in the United States and probably will continue with even stricter controls on the sanctity of water.

Wildland areas (forests and associated brush and range land) occupy a strategic position in relation to the water resources of the nation since they comprise about two-thirds of the total land area of the United States and represent the source of more than 70 percent of the nation's water yield. In addition, a major portion of these wildland watersheds is federally owned or administered.

In recent years the increasing interest in water resources has focused attention on the career field of watershed management. The term, though popularly used to describe a diversity of activities, has become nebulous and difficult to define. In its broadest sense, the scope of watershed management includes all aspects of water resources on all types of drainage basins, whether they be agricultural land, forest land, range land, urban, or complex basins. More specifically, it might be stated, that it is the effective handling of all resources of a watershed to assure maximum supplies of usable water, desirable streamflow regimes, prevention and control of erosion, and the reduction of flood and sediment damages. It is based on a thorough knowledge of how a watershed functions in receiving and disposing of precipitation, the factors that influence watershed behavior, the magnitude and limitations of their effects, and how these factors can be controlled or modified by man for his benefit.

Watershed management is the application of principles, methods, and techniques based on a thorough knowledge of the complexity of processes that influence water yield from drainage basins under various conditions of vegetation, soils, geology, physiography, and climate.

EDUCATION FOR THE PROFESSION

A person interested in a career in watershed management should have an overall understanding of the processes involved in the movement of water through the hydrologic cycle. These processes include precipitation, evaporation, transpiration, infiltration and percolation, subsurface runoff and groundwater, and surface runoff and streamflow. To understand these processes requires a good foundation in the basic sciences—mathematics, physics, and chemistry, followed by specialized education in the earth and life sciences. In addition, since water problems are often people problems, a student's educational base should also include some courses in the social sciences and humanities.

A professional career in watershed management ordinarily requires a bachelor of science degree. A career in the research or teaching phases of this field will usually require graduate study at the master's or doctoral level.

The U.S. Civil Service Commission criteria for the position of hydrologist might be used as an example of the minimum educational qualifications needed for a career in watershed management. To qualify for the entrance level position at the GS-5 grade, a student must have completed a full 4-year course of study at an accredited college or university leading to a bachelor's or higher degree with major study in physical or natural science or engineering. Course work must have included 30 semester hours in any combination of the following courses: hydrology; physical science (including geophysical sciences); engineering science; soils; mathematics; aquatic biology; or the management and conservation of water resources. The course work must have included differential and integral calculus and physics. It is anticipated that these federal requirements may become more specific in the future, and it would be wise to inquire about the current requirements before planning course work.

Few colleges and universities offer a separate curriculum leading to the bachelor's degree in watershed management because the diversity of courses required often transcends traditional department oriented curriculums. However, many universities offer degree programs with a major or option in watershed management. For instance, of the 48 colleges and universities in the United States that offer education in forestry, seven institutions offer a bachelor of science degree,

23 offer a master of science and/or master of forestry, and 18 offer a doctor of philosophy and/or doctor of forestry with a major or option in forest watershed management. Most of these curriculums have been developed through interdepartmental arrangements. In a few instances interdisciplinary degree programs are conducted under the supervision of interdepartmental committees.

The specific courses a student might be required to take will vary somewhat with the department and college in which he is enrolled. The following is an example of the types of courses a student might be required to take for a career in forest watershed management if enrolled in a school of forestry or school of natural resources:

1. *Freshman:* chemistry; algebra; trigonometry; English; botany geology; physical education; social science; speech.
2. *Sophomore:* biology; economics; statistics; soil properties; calculus; physics; technical writing; soil and water conservation; computer science; dendrology.
3. *Junior:* hydrology; forest and range ecology; forest and range management; climatology or meteorology; silviculture; forest biometrics; hydrogeology; forest soils.
4. *Senior:* Forest or watershed hydrology; watershed management; forest and range policy; water quality management; advanced hydrology; forest microclimate; forest recreation; water law; photogrammetry.

There is little opportunity for a student to specialize in an undergraduate program. Normally about three-fourths of the courses scheduled will be those required by the department for the major in which the student is enrolled. The courses taken under the watershed management option will be those taken as electives. The number of credits set aside for elective courses will vary widely between institutions.

Since the scope of watershed management cuts across so many fields of study, it is almost necessary to continue graduate study in order to specialize. This might require as much as 2 years of additional course work (30 to 45 credit hours). In addition, most universities require the preparation of a thesis or professional paper.

The specific courses scheduled by a student in a graduate program will vary with his particular interests and his career goals. For instance, a student interested in the hydrologic aspects of watershed management might take additional courses in engineering, fluid mechanics, hydraulics, and hydrometeorology. Whereas, a student interested in the vegetation management aspects might concentrate on courses in plant ecology, plant physiology, and soil science.

Rising concern over water pollution problems has increased the need for persons trained in this area. Students interested in water quality might schedule additional courses in water chemistry, water pollution control, limnology, soil chemistry, microbiology, wastewater treatment, and water quality management.

Most people working in the field of watershed management have frequent contact with the public and with federal, state, and local government officials. Hence, it is desirable for a student to include in his program some courses in the social sciences and rural sociology, humanities, public policy and administration, political science, and philosophy.

Most universities have student assistant programs available to provide financial aid to needy students from low-income families. Most institutions have scholarship and loan programs. Students entering a watershed management curriculum are usually eligible for most scholarships offered to students in the natural resource management fields. In addition, there are numerous federal aid programs administered through educational institutions. These programs, such as the Supplemental Educational Opportunity Grants, the National Direct Student Loans, and the Federal College Work-Study Programs are all available to entering freshmen.

Scholarships, fellowships, and assistantships are also available at most institutions for graduate students. Fellowships are usually granted to superior students. They are usually tax-exempt and normally do not require any service to the university.

Teaching or research assistantships are by far the most general form of financial aids given to graduate students. Assistantships are payments for services rendered to the university by students. These assistantships range from quarter-time to three-quarter-time. The award is usually subject to state and federal income taxes. At many universities the tuition costs are waived for those students working under assistantships. The half-time assistantship is the most popular and requires 20 hours of work per week. Students having assistantships must normally carry a reduced course work.

Undergraduate students who contemplate graduate study are advised to apply for fellowships or assistantships early in the fall term of their senior year. November first is the closing date each year for applications for many of the national fellowship programs. Most universities and colleges offer their assistantships during the winter term with final accepance by students by April first for the following academic year.

The increased attention being given to all aspects of water-related problems has also increased the need for technicians trained in the water resources management field. A number of 2- and 4-year technology programs are currently available. Graduates of these programs are commonly awarded technician certificates, associate degrees, or in the 4-year programs a bachelor's degree. Most of these programs are terminal and do not prepare graduates for further training or graduate study. Emphasis is usually on teaching students the practical skills required to perform duties in a rather narrow water-related field.

PERSONAL QUALIFICATIONS

Individuals with an interest in watershed management generally have an interest in nature and the outdoors, often beginning early in childhood. Perhaps this interest was stirred by living in a rural environment or through experiences in various youth organizations such as Boy Scouts, Girl Scouts, 4-H Clubs, or Future Farmers of America. This interest often manifests itself in participation in camping, fishing, hunting, hiking, and water sports. Specific interest in watershed management probably only begins to form after various outdoor experiences have brought a person face-to-face with an obvious water problem such as a fish kill, siltation of a reservoir, or a local community water shortage. These early experiences will serve an individual well if he chooses watershed management as a career since considerable amounts of field work plus a genuine desire to improve the management of our water resource are needed.

Field activities engaged in by a watershed manager vary considerably with the type of employment and the region in which he or she works. Major field activities of watershed managers are the collection of basic hydrologic data, surveys of watershed features, and supervision of construction projects to insure protection of the water resource in the present and future. With such a variety of duties, the watershed manager must be willing to deal with a broad range of subject matter spanning the physical, biological, and social sciences. Physically, being able to perform field activities is helpful. However, because of the diversity of this field, individuals with handicaps may still find satisfying employment.

The need for a broad outlook extends to the activities of the watershed manager in the office and laboratory. Computers are commonly used to compile and store the multitude of collected field data often subjected to mathematical and statistical analysis. Samples collected in the field, such as water samples for chemical quality or soil samples for texture and structure, are analyzed in the laboratory. The data collected, as well as the results of field surveys, form the base for many written and oral reports. In turn these reports are used in the formulation of watershed management plans.

Planning is perhaps the most important activity for a watershed manager since these plans guide future management of the watershed to protect and enhance the usefulness of the water resource. Here communication skills and the ability to interact with other people are of equal importance with technical knowledge.

Thus, to be an effective watershed manager, one must combine the quantitative skills of the engineer and the biologist with the communication skills of a politician. A pleasant personality is also a valuable asset to the watershed manager. Although a watershed manager initially spends a major portion of time outdoors, perhaps an equal amount of time is spent in the office, laboratory, or attending meetings. As persons advance in position they probably will also find that gradually more time is spent in the office, especially those with leadership abilities who are interested in administration.

EMPLOYMENT

Traditionally employment opportunities in watershed management have been greatest with the agencies of the federal government concerned with natural resource management and administration of public lands. This trend continues, but opportunities for watershed managers are gradually expanding in regional, state, and local government agencies, the result primarily of increased ecological awareness by the general public. The environmental movement has resulted in legislation requiring assessment of the impact of various activities, such as grazing, mining, timber harvest, and outdoor recreation, on the water resource, especially pollutant levels and the development of plans to minimize such impacts. Large private industries involved in land management have also begun to employ watershed managers for the same reasons and private consulting firms often need watershed management expertise to handle requests from smaller private firms and government agencies.

Concern with management and administration of water resources on public and private lands generally leads to the identification of water resource problems that require research before solutions can be found. Thus, opportunities exist in research primarily with federal agencies and universities. Of course, scientists at universities are also heavily involved in teaching as well as research. Demand for teachers results not only from the need to train watershed managers, but also from the need for water resource course work as part of curricula in other majors.

Federal Agencies

Many federal agencies are concerned with water resources in some way. However, several of these agencies employ the majority of practicing watershed managers. In the United States Department of Agriculture, the U.S. Forest Service and Soil Conservation Service and in the United States Department of the Interior, the U.S. Geological Survey and Bureau of Land Management employ many watershed managers. With the recent emphasis on water pollution, the Environmental Protection Agency has also been concerned with nonpoint source pollution from forest and rangeland and consequently has emerged as a watershed management employer.

The Forest Service has the responsibility for management of our national forests for multiple uses such as recreation, timber, wildlife, grazing, as well as for water. Many national forests have a watershed manager or forest hydrologist whose primary task is protecting and enhancing the water resource on the forest. Some of the activities engaged in by the watershed manager have been mentioned in the previous section to emphasize the diversity of duties.

The specific nature of such duties will vary from region to region across the United States but may include these activities: planning and supervision of road construction to prevent siltation of streams; design of sewage disposal systems from recreation areas to eliminate pollution of streams and lakes; regulation of grazing to lessen soil compaction and to decrease soil erosion; proper revegetation and reclamation of mined lands to lessen changes of water pollution; water testing to insure compliance with water quality standards, and participation in the natural resource planning process on the forest. In addition to management and administrative positions connected with the national forest system, the Forest Service also has an active research division.

The Soil Conservation Service has responsibility for implementing a national soil and water conservation program. Most employment for watershed managers with this agency involves working with individual private landowners or citizens groups to develop soil and water conservation plans on private land. In the West where most of the water for irrigation comes from snow melt, snow surveys are also conducted in the mountains each spring to help provide forecasts of water supply. The Agricultural Research Service is a research organization closely associated with the Soil Conservation Service and is responsible for research on water pollution resulting from agricultural use of the land.

The Geological Survey is responsible for monitoring the quantity and quality of water resources in the United States. Watershed managers employed by the Geological Survey generally are involved with the collection, compilation and reporting of information on the amounts and quality of water in the ground, in streams and in lakes. Work is commonly done in close association with various state agencies. The Geological Survey also is involved in research related to water resources.

The Bureau of Land Management manages public range and forest land in the West with responsibilities quite similar to those of the Forest Service. Grazing, mining, timber harvesting, recreational use, and wildlife production are all uses of the land managed by this agency. These activities are coordinated by watershed managers to protect the water resources. Both land management and structural practices are used to protect the water resource on these lands.

The Environmental Protection Agency (EPA) was created in 1970 as a regulatory agency responsible for establishing and enforcing environmental standards including those needed to protect our nation's resources. One of the major sources of water pollution, identified by EPA, is the so called "nonpoint source" pollution produced by gradual additions of a pollutant from farm, range, or forest land. This is opposed to "point source" pollution resulting from direct discharge from a factory or waste treatment plant through a pipe or ditch into a lake or stream. Because of this concern for nonpoint source pollution, some watershed managers can expect to find employment with the EPA especially as researchers in EPA laboratories established throughout the United States.

Other federal agencies which may occasionally employ watershed managers are the Bureau of Indian Affairs and Bureau of Reclamation in the Department of the Interior, the U.S. Department of Defense, Army Corps of Engineers, and the Tennessee Valley Authority.

Regional, State and Local Agencies

Various government agencies at the regional, state, or local level employ watershed managers. Employment, typically at the administrative level, can be found with various regional agencies such as the large river basin commissions which usually span several states in their jurisdictions. Each state also usually employs a small watershed management staff as part of the state natural resources, conservation, or forestry department. Local governments of the larger cities where the water supply comes from a local watershed often employ watershed managers to manage the watershed lands for multiple uses while protecting and enhancing the water supply. Smaller cities often rely on consulting services rather than employing their own watershed manager.

Private Business

Although the demand is not great, some industries and consulting firms employ watershed managers. Industries likely to be interested in watershed managers are the larger forest products firms and private water companies. With a large forest products firm, a watershed manager is typically needed to insure that timber management activities do not adversely affect the water resource on company lands or on adjoining lands. Similarly, private water companies must be sure that their water supply is not jeopardized by other uses of the watershed lands.

Consulting firms involved in engineering or environmental studies for clients are also potential employers of watershed managers. Often the role of the watershed manager in a consulting firm is to help with an overall assessment of the impact of a construction project on the environment. The watershed manager may also establish his own consulting business involved with impact assessment and development of watershed management plans.

Students interested in a teaching career may want to pursue a Ph.D. degree with ultimate employment with a university. Experience in management and administration is desirable before accepting a teaching position. Some of the schools with teaching positions in watershed management are listed in Appendix A. The trend has been for each forestry school to employ at least one specialist in watershed management.

In addition to these sources of employment, foreign opportunities for watershed managers are gradually increasing with the United Nations either through volunteer programs such as the Peace Corps or staff positions with the Food and Agriculture Organization (FAO). International employment with FAO usually requires fluency in another language, field experience, and an advanced degree. Often field experience and fluency in a foreign language can be obtained in a volunteer position followed by regular employment with FAO.

Estimates of the current numbers of watershed management specialists employed are not available. Approximately 350 members of the 17,000-member Society of American Foresters belong to the Hydrology and Meteorology Working Group which indicates that forest watershed specialists are a small fraction of the forestry profession. Since other professions also include the field of watershed management, the total number of watershed specialists employed is possibly only about 500, or at least less than 1,000.

Future employment opportunities in the field of watershed management is difficult to predict because of the high proportion of

graduates employed by the federal government. Federal hiring policies vary with the economic policies of each administration which
largely control the job market for watershed managers. Regardless,
the *demand* for watershed managers is likely to increase with continued public interest in environmental issues. Expanded mining of
our nation's mineral resources on public lands to meet the energy crisis
will no doubt contribute to the increased demand. Although the proportion of graduates employed by the nonfederal sector is smaller,
the trend has been promising with a gradually expanding employment
base. Generally, a student completing an undergraduate degree in a
natural resource field, followed by specialized training in watershed
management at the master's degree level can expect to find satisfying
employment in this field. Individuals attaining the Ph.D. degree can
usually find employment in teaching or research.

COMPENSATION AND REWARDS

Most students interested in a career in watershed management do so
because of their desire to work in the out-of-doors. There is, of
course, much personal satisfaction in being able to work with nature.
Work in the field of watershed management can often take one into
rural and wilderness areas, particularly those specializing in forest
watershed management. Such assignments may have a romantic at-
traction for the single employee or married couple with no children.

In all probability, a starting employee would spend much of his
or her time in the field. As he or she grows professional more time
would probably be spent in a laboratory or an office. Federal research
centers are often located in college communities. Government agencies are becoming more aware of the fact that young professional
employees with families are happier when they are located near good
schools, churches, libraries, medical facilities, and other cultural and
social amenities.

Generally, the income of a person employed in the field of
watershed management is comparable to that of a professional forester, soil scientist, or civil engineer. Because the field is so diversified,
there are many opportunities for advancement. As in almost any
career field, professional and financial advancement will depend on
both technical competence and personal characteristics.

Water is an integral part of everyone's life. As a consequence, the work of the watershed management specialist will often be exposed to public scrutiny. He or she should be willing to participate in community projects. Although the job may be frustrating at times, the career person will always have the satisfaction of contributing to the conservation and wise management of our most valuable resource —water.

10 Wildlife Biology and Management

FRED G. EVENDEN

During man's early times on earth, wildlife provided food, clothing, utensils, and shelter, and sometimes was a source of danger or competition. In recent centuries, other natural resources have been developed, reducing man's dependence on wildlife for his existence. Although wildlife still plays a subsistence role in some primitive human cultures, most of modern man's interest in wildlife has turned toward recreational, commercial, artistic, and aesthetic values. However, wildlife still competes with some of man's activities, such as crop production.

In America the subsistence use of wildlife by natives lessened as white settlers spread over the continent. As the white man's affluence, knowledge, and mechanization grew, his dependence on personally harvested wildlife for food and clothing was reduced, although wild meats, furs, and hides were still harvested for the commercial market. Market hunting gradually ceased as wildlife populations were reduced or crowded out by man's axes, plows, guns, dams, and homes.

Serious concern for America's wildlife developed late in the nineteenth century as citizen conservation groups combined their efforts to halt its abuse and reduction. Federal, state, provincial, and private agencies were created to conserve wildlife, and management programs were developed. By the 1920s it was recognized that special skills and knowledge were required to apply proper wildlife management techniques. Special courses were offered in a few universities and colleges to meet these needs. As more wildlife biologists and management specialists were educated, they formed a professional association, The Wildlife Society, in 1937.

The profession's early orientation toward education, research, and management was focused on the so-called game forms of wildlife. Many Americans who supported wildlife conservation with their own time and money were primarily interested in game species. They engaged in an uphill struggle between wildlife's needs and increasing human expansion. Early management efforts were successful for many wildlife species, although the passenger pigeon and the heath hen had become extinct. Fortunately, many wildlife species were brought back to abundance, among them the white-tailed deer, pronghorn antelope, beaver, and wild turkey. These early efforts used harvest regulation, habitat preservation in refuges, and artificial propagation.

Interest in wildlife has broadened during recent years to include all wildlife, whether or not it is harvested. This interest has brought about federal, state, and provincial laws for the protection of nongame and endangered species. It places new responsibilities on wildlife scientists and managers.

EDUCATION FOR THE PROFESSION

The personal interests and talents one possesses will influence the wildlife educational route to be chosen. Education for a wildlife career can encompass a combination of diverse disciplines or be limited to a single specialty, although such narrowness may be a disadvantage in the professional's future.

Most of those working with wildlife resources today entered the field with a broad biological background, enhanced by an understanding of the practical application of that knowledge based on field experience. Some work in wildlife because of their expertise in other specialties, such as administration, chemistry, communications, or electronics. Many diverse disciplines often are combined in a team effort to solve management problems.

Wildlife biologists collecting and preparing pheasants for transplanting to another habitat. (Photo by U.S. Fish and Wildlife Service.)

Those universities and colleges (see Appendix A) offering curricula specializing in wildlife biology and resources management built their programs on biological course requirements, and most degrees have a science base. Recent curricula changes reflect recognition of the expanding role of wildlife management with other disciplines, particularly those in socioeconomics. In other words, beyond the initial acquisition of scientific knowledge and processes, a successful wildlife resource manager works with people. Economics, politics, law, public relations, and a host of other human activities and needs are each involved in the environment in which satisfactory management results must be achieved.

Some educational institutions may be better for one wildlife specialty than another because of their professional staff and their specialties, because of their geographical location, or because of the size and status of departmental facilities and equipment for instruction or research.

What constitutes a minimum degree for training as a wildlife resources professional? Most wildlife professionals would agree that a bachelor's degree is basic and suffices for many technician and entrance level positions. Increasingly, however, we find that the successful applicants for positions have educational qualifications beyond the bachelor's level. A projection of this trend indicates clearly that the master's degree soon will become the education level for entrance to the wildlife profession.

The Wildlife Society has recommended a minimum course credit criteria for a bachelor's degree in wildlife. A 1977 revision of those recommended criteria include as minimum educational requirements a full four-year course of study in an accredited college or university leading to a bachelor's or higher degree in wildlife with at least the following course requirements:

1. *36 semester hours in biological sciences*, which must include:

    (*a*) *24 semester hours* in basic biological courses such as general botany, general zoology, mammalogy, ornithology, genetics, physiology, anatomy, plant ecology, animal ecology, taxonomy, or behavior.

    (*b*) *6 semester hours*, in courses such as principles and practices of wildlife management.

    (*c*) *6 semester hours*, in related courses such as biology (ecology) of birds or mamals, forestry, fisheries science, or range management.

2. *9 semester hours in physical sciences*, such as chemistry, physics, geology or soils, with at least two subject areas represented.

3. *9 semester hours in quantitative sciences*, which must include:

    (*a*) *3 semester hours* in statistics.

    (*b*) *6 semester hours* in courses such as algebra, calculus, computer science, systems analysis, or mathematical modeling.

4. *9 semester hours in humanities and social sciences*, such as economics, sociology, psychology, political science, government, history, or literature.

5. *12 semester hours in communications*, such as English composition, technical writing, journalism, public speaking, or use of mass media.

6. *6 semester hours in policy, administration, or law*, such as resource policy and/or administration, environmental law, law enforcement, or land-use planning.

Student enrollments have increased to a point where graduates in the 1970s have found wildlife employment opportunities very competitive. Periodic surveys by the Wildlife Society (*The Wildlife Society News*, Nos. 123, 127, and 138; *Wildlife Society Bulletin*, Vol. 2, No. 2, and Vol. 5 in press) show placement success in wildlife and wildlife-related positions for degree earners as follows: bachelor's, 26-50 percent; master's, 65-75 percent; and doctor's, 85-98 percent. These figures reflect an oversupply of graduates for available positions.

The Wildlife Society adopted in 1977 a program for voluntary certification of wildlife biologists. This program should help the professional more effectively to manage and perpetuate the wildlife resources in the face of massive, highly diverse problems that arise daily.

Costs of obtaining an education continue to rise. Undergraduates may seek assistance through their chosen university, through student aid programs, state and federal loans, and through major industrial and foundation scholarship programs. Scholarships and graduate research and teaching assistanceships often are available to graduate students, and must be sought at the university chosen by the student. Some scholarship programs for wildlife students are sponsored annually by a number of national associations.

PERSONAL QUALIFICATIONS

A few decades ago, one trained in wildlife management, physically strong, and male had the personal qualifications necessary for a career in this field. Time, professional development, and sophistication of equipment have changed all that. No longer do a majority of wildlife positions require great physical strength, although some work activities cannot be performed without it. Since some work requires a capability to adjust to unusual or adverse living conditions, generally good health will be a benefit. Women are now employed in every aspect of wildlife resources management.

Wildlife resources management is largely "people management." Knowing the facts and knowing what to do with them are not enough. Getting proposed management techniques accepted by decision-makers, creating public awareness and public support, obtaining necessary funding, and then monitoring satisfactions and benefits received are all important.

Wildlife scientists must be trained in biology and understand natural ecological interrelationships. However, not all of them can interpret ecological concepts beyond the natural environment. Full success for their management proposals may be in the hands of other decision-makers who must consider economic, legal, and social factors, as well as public opinion.

Anyone entering the field, in addition to being intelligent, well-educated, professionally skilled, diligent and patient, must like people, be communicative, be willing to work with a diversity of human personalities, and be dedicated to working toward a secure future for wildlife resources.

EMPLOYMENT

Historically, career employment in wildlife resources was largely limited to government agencies, colleges, and universities. Private employment opportunities were few.

Although government agencies still predominate in wildlife employment, opportunities have expanded at local government levels and in the private sector.

A wide choice of careers is open under a variety of conditions, including those as wildlife resources manager or researcher on land or sea, administrator, artist, information specialist, professor, educator, enforcement officer, computer or electronics specialist, land-use planner, naturalist, land acquisition specialist, and consultant. Although these may appear highly specialized, experience has shown that a broad and diverse background and rigorous education will help a wildlifer do a good job in a chosen speciality, whatever it may be. Review of principal work areas follows:

Wildlife Management

With a well-balanced technical background, the wildlifer might work directly with wild animals and their environments. Thus one might concentrate on different forms or groups of wildlife, aquatic or terrestrial, game or nongame, endangered or overabundant species. One might manage refuges or public recreation areas, establish harvest regulations, make surveys, count or "census" populations, increase or reduce populations, or evaluate and improve habitat. One could work with foresters or other resource managers to develop integrated plans for natural resources management. Later on, with experience, this work could lead to broader activities.

Wildlife Research

Successful wildlife management is based on facts obtained by scientific research. Wildlife biologists, particularly those with master or doctoral degrees, perform research to obtain facts on such subjects as habitat relations, physiology, ecology, disease, nutrition, population dynamics, land-use changes, and pollution. A research scientist must be inquisitive, patient, and persistent, be able to collect, analyze, and interpret facts with objectivity and proficiency, and must be able to communicate them clearly to other researchers, managers, and the general public.

Wildlife and Public Relations

Those in public relations interpret research and management efforts to promote understanding, agency image and credibility, and acceptance of recommendations and policies. This work involves writing articles or pamphlets and news releases, photography, public speaking, and cooperation with press, radio, and television. New illustrative material about wildlife is always needed for training and educational purposes. Abilities in photography or art can be valuable in a public relations career. For public relations work, one obviously needs talent, imagination, and effective communication skills combined with a technical wildlife background and a genuine liking for people.

Wildlife Education

Opportunities to teach wildlife ecology and management were most numerous at the universities, but there is now an increasing need for teachers with a wildlife background in elementary and secondary schools, especially in science or ecology-related programs.

Extension is another arm of education through which technical assistance in wildlife resources management is offered to individuals and groups. Effective extension work requires a special willingness to work with people in addition to an understanding of farm, forest, urban, and industrial land uses and economics, plus practical experience in wildlife management. A wildlife extension specialist may explain the results of research to persons and groups who need and should have correct and up-to-date information on wildlife resources. There are all too few such positions in existence today.

Wildlife Law Enforcement

Wildlife management also involves the enforcement of laws and regulations designed to maintain optimum wildlife populations. Today's more progressive enforcement or conservation officer, in addition to enforcing the law, may count animals, control wildlife populations, recommend hunting seasons, and may be a wildlife manager or educator as well. Special enforcement training obviously is required. The modern enforcement officer also strives to enlighten the public regarding conservation laws, management practices, and improved sportsmanship.

Recreation

Outdoor recreation is increasingly an important part of human activity. Wildlife is not only important to those who hunt and fish, but also to those, such as bird watchers, who simply enjoy observing and studying wildlife as an interesting part of the natural scene. The land-management agencies of state, provincial, and federal governments, plus private agencies, need persons who can handle recreationists whether they are equipped with wheels, fishing rods, guns, cameras, or binoculars.

Land-Use Planning

Wildlife professionals may provide leadership in well-balanced environmental land-use planning, that is, planning for all natural resources. Broad training is essential in this diverse field.

Administration

All organizations, agencies, and institutions must be led, coordinated, and administered. Administration is a specialized function. It usually requires a person who has risen through the professional ranks, knows the field, and has a facility for working with people.

In addition to technical knowledge, a good sense of public relations and business management is essential, for many administrative problems involve either people or budgets. An administrator must be able to develop and sell a sound resources management program, since most budgets are approved and funds allocated by those who must consider many competing priorities for funds.

Consultant

During the broadened environmental movement of the 1960s came the National Environmental Policy Act of 1969 (NEPA). The impact of NEPA is only now being widely recognized. It establishes a legal system for ensuring a quality environment. This act requires federal, state, and private agencies and groups proposing major actions that will significantly alter the environment on public lands must analyze and report the likely effects of the proposed actions on the environment. That word "report" opened a new field for independent wildlife professionals who make their services available as private consultants. Business, industry, and government need experienced wildlife consultants to assist with fulfillment of NEPA's requirements. Passage of parallel legislation in many states has broadened consultant opportunities.

Public Agencies

Most wildlife-oriented positions are with state, provincial, or federal agencies. Usually they are under civil service. Positions such as wildlife biologist, game manager, park naturalist, research biologist, and conservation officer (some states and provinces excepted) require at least a bachelor's degree and entrance examinations.

State or provincial agencies include departments of conservation, natural resources, wildlife, fish and game, forestry, and parks and recreation. United States agencies include the Fish and Wildlife Service, National Marine Fisheries Service, Forest Service, National Park Service, Bureau of Land Management, Bureau of Outdoor Recreation, Bureau of Reclamation, Soil Conservation Service, Council on Environmental Quality, Environmental Protection Agency, Corps of Engineers, and all other branches of the Department of Defense. In Canada, the provincial governments and the Canadian Department of the Environment (Wildlife, Fisheries and Marine, and Forestry Services) are major employers.

Many county, town and city agencies now employ wildlife management specialists as well.

Colleges and Universities

Universities and colleges offering a wildlife curriculum employ wildlife professionals for their teaching staff and research programs. Professors specializing in wildlife biology usually perform research as well as teach and need a broad academic background in science, humanities, and technical subjects. They should have an understanding of the theoretical, as well as practical, principles of ecology, management and administration. A doctorate is usually essential.

Private

Opportunities in private employment have expanded rapidly since enactment of the National Environmental Policy Act of 1969. Engineering and other consulting firms now employ wildlife specialists. A wildlife biologist with sufficient background, knowledge, experience, and an excellent reputation may become a self-employed consultant.

Private employment with large firms dealing in timber, ranching, mining, crop or energy production, and with firms producing paper or chemicals is also increasing. Other opportunities exist in game farming, fish farming, and with sportsmen's clubs.

One might also earn a living as a writer, artist, or photographer specializing in wildlife. Each year there are increasing opportunities in community nature or conservation centers and zoos, and in a growing number of private and public conservation-related organizations throughout the world.

SATISFACTIONS AND REWARDS

Although a love of wild animals and nature may have enticed one to choose a wildlife resources field for a career, a thorough reading of this chapter certainly should be convincing evidence that achieving that career will not be easy. If one expects an idylic life in the outdoors, such an expectation may be fleeting, for as one advances in this profession, the chances are that he or she will see less and less of that great outdoors.

A career in wildlife resources demands extensive preparation, long hours of hard work to acquire knowledge and skills, fierce competition for employment, and a dogged determination toward personal goals. One must overcome the frustrations and disappointments of working with wild populations, with limited budgets, and with low political and social priorities for wildlife.

Compensation for most wildlife workers is guided by the civil service salary schedules of the public agencies under which the majority of positions occur. Salaries are competitive but not high, and, in many wildlife positions, these salaries may not be immediately commensurate with the time and money invested in career preparation.

The current salary status of federal, state, provincial, or university wildlife starting positions may be obtained from their offices. Often the salaries of state and provincial positions are lower than in federal agencies, and salary levels vary greatly between the states and the provinces for equivalent positions. Once one has passed the major hurdle of initial employment in a chosen profession and has gained experience, there are opportunities to advance in responsibility.

"Compensation in the Fields of Fish and Wildlife Management" is published annually by the National Wildlife Federation. This report not only summarizes current trends, but also provides comparisons among numerous positions in the principal federal agencies employing wildlife professionals, in colleges and universities, and in each of the 50 states.

Those who work in wildlife resources management with a sincere sense of dedication will find the rewards are much more than salary. Major additional bonuses to dedicated workers include the personal satisfaction received, the privilege that one may have to work outdoors, and the knowledge that one is playing a vital role in the wise stewardship of man's heritage of wildlife and other natural resources for the future.

11 Biology

HENRY CLEPPER

Biology, the science of life, embraces three broad areas: zoology or animal sciences, botany or plant sciences, and microbiology or the science of microorganisms. Biologists who work in the fields of natural resource conservation and management are mainly concerned with botany (as in forestry and range management) and zoology (as in fisheries and wildlife management).

But there are many specialties, called disciplines, in which biologists have the skills and knowledge that are essential to the scientific management of natural resources. For example, biologists specialize in entomology (insects), ichthyology (fish), mammalogy (mammals), and ornithology (birds).

In the plant resources, biologists contribute their knowledge to agronomy (the relationship between soil and crop production), silviculture (the growing of tree crops), plant pathology (the science of plant diseases), mycology (fungi), plant physiology (the study of the function and behavior of plants), plant taxonomy (description, classification, and study of the interrelationships of the members of the plant kingdom), plant morphology (study of the form and structure of plants), horticulture (fruit and vegetable crops as well as ornamental plants), and bryology (mosses and liverworts).

These are only a few of the kinds of disciplines in which biologists work. Others are genetics (the study and application of heredity mechanisms, so important in the development of superior forest trees), marine biology (the study of life in the seas), limnology (the study

of life in lakes and streams), and the broad area of ecology (the interactions of organisms with one another and with their environment).
Ecologists who are working for the improvement of environmental
quality are among the most useful practitioners in the nation.

Opportunities for biologists in natural resources are expanding in
many fields, particularly in those concerned with changes in the environment. Air, water, and soil pollution abatement, for example, has
become so prominent in the past decade that numerous governmental
and industrial agencies have been created to handle this great social
and economic crisis. Pollution control is not work for biologists alone,
however. Increasingly, they collaborate with economists, engineers,
medical doctors, physicists, officers of government, toxicologists, and
other workers in related occupations. As we become more concerned
about preservation of our renewable resources and total environment,
there will be new professions and technician positions where adapt-
ability and familiarity with other disciplines will be an advantage.

Hence, it is evident that the professional biologist working in
natural resource conservation is both a specialist and a generalist. He
or she may be expected to be experienced not only in his or her area
of competence—limnology, let us say—but also to know something
about hydrology, geology, and meteorology as well.

EDUCATIONAL REQUIREMENTS

How does one become a biologist? High school students must have
a foundation in basic subjects before entering college. Because the
biologist must be a good communicator, the student must be well
versed in English, in speech, writing, and comprehensive reading.
Governmental and industrial employers customarily demand that
biologists, especially those in the growing field of environmental improvement, be skilled in oral and written communication. Competence
in mathematics is equally essential for mathematics is a tool in biological research.

A high school graduate who has successfully completed the
science courses will be qualified to enroll in a college-level biology
curriculum.

A bachelor's degree is the minimum academic qualification for

A tree geneticist places protective sacks over pine cones a year after controlled pollination. (Photo by U.S. Forest Service.)

the professional biologist. This basic degree can be obtained at most of the hundreds of universities and colleges in America. For the undergraduate student, any accredited institution should provide a suitable curriculum. Many college students take a wide variety of courses during the first two years and specialize in the biology major during the last two. Most biology majors have minored in chemistry, mathematics, or physics, though a recent trend indicates many are minoring in anthropology, sociology, or psychology.

Students intending to work for the master's or doctor's degree might wish to attend institutions that are recognized as specializing in the particular curriculums desired, for example, botany, ecology, genetics, ichthyology, or plant pathology and entomology. Information about such leading universities is usually obtained during the student's undergraduate period.

In general, graduates with the best academic preparation may expect to have the best job opportunities, the best salaries, and the best rewards in job satisfactions.

Although academic background always will be a factor in ac-

ceptance at college and in later employment, there is another pre-
liminary to a career which should not be overlooked. This is the
nature of summer employment and the part-time work during the
school year. There are many ways in which to obtain an exposure to
the worlds of biology, such as working in nurseries, orchards, parks,
and conservation programs in one's own community. Such employment provides experience in some of the applied aspects of one's
choice of professions. On occasion, a student might find that the real
application is not at all what has been anticipated. It is equally possible
that one will find the experience satisfying and challenging to the
point that the decision to continue training for that profession is
firmer. Employers are paying increasing attention to the nature of
summer employment undertaken during school years as an indication
of both interest and initiative.

THE WORK OF THE BIOLOGIST

Biologists in natural resources can look forward to interesting and
useful employment. Those who work in outdoor environments may
travel to forests, mountains, plains, oceans, lakes, rivers, and indeed
every corner of the nation. Others, engaged in research, may make
their discoveries in laboratories. Some work alone. Many work in
teams or groups, either with fellow biologists or with professionals in
other disciplines.

Many are teachers, either in high schools or in institutions of
higher learning, especially professional schools. Many are employed
by government departments and bureaus. Their work may be in national and state forests and parks, oceanographic agencies, fisheries
and wildlife services, and range conservation and soil conservation
operations. A considerable number of industries now employ biologists as natural resource conservationists and as field research workers.

Some jobs require strenuous outdoor exertion, often in extreme
weather conditions. Although it was once assumed that only men
could work in, and endure, such conditions, it has since been proved
that women are also competent in such environments.

Here are a few examples of the many kinds of work biologists
perform in natural resource conservation and management. It is to be

noted that these are only a sampling and that the examples could be extended a hundred-fold.

In fisheries biology, one studies diseases of fish in hatcheries where fish are raised for stocking of lakes, streams, and other waters. Fish are subject to diseases as are all forms of animal life, and some biologists specialize in the prevention and cure of such diseases. A related problem that fisheries biologists must contend with is the bloom of poisonous microscopic animals and plants that sometimes occurs in sea waters.

Forest lands cover approximately one quarter of the land area in the United States and forest entomologists are employed in most forested regions to detect and control the many insect pests that damage and destroy valuable timber stands. About three quarters of all species of animals in the world today are insects, and few people realize more timber is lost to insects than to forest fires. Among the most destructive insects are the spruce budworm, the tussock moth, the gypsy moth, and the larch sawfly. Bark beetles are perhaps the most destructive of all insects with regard to the extent and volume of standing timber ruined.

With the existence of more than 50,000 destructive plant diseases which continually threaten to cause shortages of food and building supplies, plant pathologists are among the most important guardians of our forests and rangelands. They must cope with parasitic diseases caused by fungi, viruses, nematodes, and mistletoes. The destructive chestnut blight, introduced into the United States in 1904, spread throughout the natural range of the native chestnut tree and during the past seventy years wiped it out. But another destructive fungi— the white pine blister rust—can be controlled, and biologists have found ways to do it.

The biological control of weeds on rangelands is an important function of range management. One method of control is to introduce or encourage insects to reduce the reproduction of noxious plants. A successful example was the importation into the United States of a beetle whose larvae eat the plant known as Klamath weed or goatweed, which has spread extensively over the northewestern states.

Without the contributions of biologists, notably the research workers in their laboratories, the conservation and management of our renewable natural resources would not be as far advanced as they are today.

COMPENSATION AND SATISFACTIONS

Compensation received by biologists employed in natural resources is comparable to that paid other professionals and scientists, such as engineers, foresters, fisheries, range, and wildlife managers, and soil conservationists. As previously mentioned, salaries are usually keyed to the level of education. All other things being equal, income and position are higher for biologists with advanced degrees and advanced education, especially for those in teaching and research. Historically, salaries have been rising, and may be expected to continue to rise.

But the appeal of money should not be the only goal or even the main one. Most biologists find that their contributions to society are useful and appreciated, both by their peers and by the public. This observation holds for the biologist who stays in a technical field, such as research in genetics, or the one who moves into administration.

Biology's great diversity assures the young biologist that career opportunities are many and the satisfactions great.

12 Land Use

KENNETH P. DAVIS

Land, its uses, ownership, and controls is of basic social and economic importance to people. They not only live on a finite amount of land but are dependent on its many resources for sustenance. Basically, the more people there are, the more intensive are the pressures on the land and consequent need for control of its many uses.

The scope of land use, past and present, is too broad and varied to be identified with a particular academic profession. The reason is that applications are too many and varied to fit a specific curriculum pattern.

Probably one of the oldest planned applications of land use, other than agricultural and urban, dates back to landscape architecture which developed on English country estates. The term was coined in the United States by Frederick Law Olmsted in the 1800s. It has been applied to scenic parkways in the United States, such as the Blue Ridge Parkway Skyline Drive, the Natchez Trace Highway (U.S. 40), the Wilbur Cross-Merritt Parkway in Connecticut, and to many scenic trails and walkways.

The general principles of, and need for, good land use planning apply to construction and maintenance of interstate and other highways, national, state, and other parks, and the management of agricultural, grazing, and forest lands in both public and private ownership.

They also equally apply to urban land use planning and zoning in many forms and applications ranging from building skyscrapers to housing developments, with all of which careful and good design of land use is extremely important.

124

Modern development of land use in the United States can be characterized as a concomitant of a growing population placing increasing pressure on a finite amount of land. There is consequent need to use this land well and to recognize both utilitarian and aesthetic considerations.

EDUCATION FOR THE PROFESSION

To repeat, land use cannot be clearly identified as a particular profession and particularly so from an academic standpoint. There are few if any academic curriculums, none to the writer's knowledge, that use a land use title. The reason is that "land use" is an extremely broad and general term drawing a wide range of academic disciplines. Basically, a broad education is needed.

Because of this, treatment here will deal broadly with school and curriculum offerings within a university or other qualified educational unit. Institutions will not be named since they vary widely in organization, educational emphasis, content, direction, and character of advanced courses. The student will need to inquire about the particular nature, kind, level, and quality of desired courses.

Concerning professional and educational units with major curriculums or courses relating to land use, the following may be useful depending on particular interests:

The American Institute of Planners, Washington, D.C. This is a well-known organization of high reputation.

Forestry schools and curriculums which are professionally oriented. They are deeply concerned with large scale land use.

Botanical and biological courses. These are offered in most academic institutions, and give necessary background for land use in practice, including tree and plant identification and nurture, the nature and control of destructive insects and other biota.

Civil engineering. Knowledge here is needed in land use in a number of ways, including water drainage, water needs and control problems, and design and construction of roads and trails and their maintenance. A general durability and flexibility of mind is valuable in land use because of its varied nature and requirements.

It is not possible, at present at any rate, to give the number of

These federal officers are engaged in land use planning to determine the area's suitability for skiing. (Photo by U.S. Forest Service.)

universities specifically offering a land use program because of reasons stated. It is not generally considered as a particular curriculum. Just the same, a student can find the courses to emphasize a land use oriented program at most of the major institutions. No particular previous specialization is needed, but a student must meet the general educational entrance qualifications of the institution.

The student will need to inquire about scholarships, fellowships, and assistantships. Submission of previous academic records and other pertinent information is required in advance of admission. It is also desirable to visit the school in person before entering as a student and to ask about particular programs and academic requirements which may have a bearing on the student's academic desires.

PERSONAL QUALIFICATIONS

The practice of land use is, by its nature, broad and varied. It is of concern to many people who often feel strongly about uses of land both generally and personally.

Practitioners need to have or develop a broad outlook and balance, an integrative sense, and a liking and understanding of people. Controversy is endemic to the practice of land use.

Workers in land use should be able to deal with technical and physical matters relative to their interests. The kind and degree vary greatly according to the situation. For example, urban land use planning, which can range from urban housing development to skyscrapers, is quite different from agriculture or large scale forest land use. But these certainly do involve land use although in different contexts. A college graduate cannot be expected to have a high level of particular expertise to start with. But he or she should be willing to study and learn by practice and through others. Land use is an area of action and concern and not a particular dicipline. It is too varied to define specific personal and physical requirements or particular skills needed.

EMPLOYMENT

Land use, since it is a broad area of concern, offers a wide range of employment.

They can include employment with public agencies, such as the U.S. Forest Service, Bureau of Land Management, state, county, and urban units, industrial organizations concerned with land uses, and self-employment as consultants in both urban and nonurban areas.

Kinds of work can include natural resource management, administration, and a wide range of technical work. Also particular areas such as tree regeneration by planting or seeding, studies in and control of various insects and plant diseases both in the laboratory and the field, and a range of urban situations and problems are part of land use. A great deal of research and other technical work is also done that relates to land use. But because it is a broad rather than a specific discipline it is difficult, in a general description like this chapter, to identify particular jobs in detail. But since it is a large field of much importance, land use has the advantage of a wide range of employment opportunities.

Women are professionally employed in land use areas. Jobs range from active field work such as ground land management, research of many kinds, and administrative responsibilities at various levels. Clerical service is not included here but many women do clerical service in land use oriented organizations. As far as this writer knows there is no barrier against minority people. They can get jobs as their ability merits.

Because of the wide scope of land use and increasing public concern about how land is used, it does not seem that the professional area is overcrowded. Many jobs do and will exist in land use and they are likely to increase in the future. Consequently this writer does not believe that job overcrowding is likely.

COMPENSATION AND REWARDS

Land use will be an increasing area of professional concern because of the basic fact that more and more people are filling a finite amount of land and its many natural resources.

For this reason compensation should not fall behind that received in comparable professional work.

As for satisfactions and standing, work in the land use area should rate rather high because it deals with an area of basic and continuing interest and importance to many people.

APPENDIXES

Appendix A

UNIVERSITIES AND COLLEGES

Universities and colleges in the United States that offer curriculums and degree programs in the various fields of natural resource conservation are listed by subjects, below. In writing to any of these institutions, the prospective student might inquire whether they issue descriptive literature about the curriculum or program; many do so.

ENVIRONMENTAL CONSERVATION

Environmental conservation does not have a standard educational curriculum. College programs in this field have a variety of names, such as environmental studies, environmental management, resource conservation, as well as environmental conservation. Students usually put their academic programs together under faculty guidance.

CALIFORNIA POLYTECHNIC STATE UNIVERSITY, San Luis Obispo, CA 93401.
UNIVERSITY OF CALIFORNIA, Berkeley, CA   94720.
UNIVERSITY OF CALIFORNIA, Davis, CA   95616.
UNIVERSITY OF CALIFORNIA, Los Angeles, CA   90024.
UNIVERSITY OF CALIFORNIA, Santa Cruz, CA   95060.
UNIVERSITY OF SOUTHERN CALIFORNIA, Los Angeles, CA   90007.
UNIVERSITY OF NEW HAVEN, West Haven, CT   06516.
GEORGE WASHINGTON UNIVERSITY, Washington, DC   20006.
GEORGIA COLLEGE, Milledgeville, GA   31061.
UNIVERSITY OF ILLINOIS, Urbana, IL   61801.
BALL STATE UNIVERSITY, Muncie, IN   47306.
INDIANA UNIVERSITY, Bloomington, IN   47401.

KANSAS STATE UNIVERSITY, Manhattan, KS   66502.

EASTERN KENTUCKY UNIVERSITY, Richmond, KY   40475.

MOREHEAD STATE UNIVERSITY, Morehead, KY   40351.

McNEESE STATE UNIVERSITY, Lake Charles, LA   70601.

UNIVERSITY OF MARYLAND, College Park, MD   20742.

SPRINGFIELD COLLEGE, Springfield, MA   01109.

EASTERN MICHIGAN UNIVERSITY, Ypsilanti, MI   48197.

UNIVERSITY OF MICHIGAN, Ann Arbor, MI   48104.

WESTERN MICHIGAN UNIVERSITY, Kalamazoo, MI   49001.

BEMIDJI STATE UNIVERSITY, Bemidji, MN   56601.

UNIVERSITY OF SOUTHERN MISSISSIPPI, Hattiesburg, MS   39401.

UNIVERSITY OF NEW HAMPSHIRE, Durham, NH   03824.

MONTCLAIR STATE COLLEGE, Upper Montclair, NJ   07043.

CORNELL UNIVERSITY, Ithaca, NY   14850.

STATE UNIVERSITY OF NEW YORK, COLLEGE OF ENVIRONMENTAL SCIENCE
AND FORESTRY, Syracuse, NY   13210.

DUKE UNIVERSITY, Durham, NC   27706.

NORTH CAROLINA STATE UNIVERSITY, Raleigh, NC   27607.

ANTIOCH COLLEGE, Yellow Springs, OH   45387.

BOWLING GREEN STATE UNIVERSITY, Bowling Green, OH   43403.

UNIVERSITY OF AKRON, Akron, OH   44325.

DREXEL UNIVERSITY, Philadelphia, PA   19104.

PENNSYLVANIA STATE UNIVERSITY, University Park, PA   16802.

SLIPPERY ROCK STATE COLLEGE, Slippery Rock, PA   16057.

RICE UNIVERSITY, Houston, TX   77001.

STEPHEN F. AUSTIN STATE UNIVERSITY, Nacogdoches, TX   75961.

TEXAS CHRISTIAN UNIVERSITY, Fort Worth, TX   76129.

UNIVERSITY OF VERMONT, Burlington, VT   05401.

VIRGINIA POLYTECHNIC INSTITUTE AND STATE UNIVERSITY, Blacksburg,
VA   24061.

WASHINGTON STATE UNIVERSITY, Pullman, WA   99163.

WESTERN WASHINGTON STATE COLLEGE, Bellingham, WA   98225.

UNIVERSITY OF WISCONSIN, Green Bay, WI   54305.

SOIL CONSERVATION

Degrees in soil conservation and related disciplines can be earned at
all state land-grant colleges. Most land-grant colleges have (1) a
resident teaching staff for the college curriculum, (2) a state agricul-

tural experiment station for research, and (3) a liberal arts curriculum for electives in communication, economics, political science, and other fields of study important in working with the public.

For programs available at other colleges and universities, obtain a catalog of courses to determine whether or not the scientific and technical programs are adequate. Many colleges in recent years have added to their environmental and conservation study programs.

OUTDOOR RECREATION

Colleges and universities offering resource-oriented, degree curriculums in outdoor recreation management; listed alphabetically by states.

ARIZONA STATE UNIVERSITY, Tempe, AZ   85281.
UNIVERSITY OF ARIZONA, Tucson, AZ   85721.
NORTHERN ARIZONA UNIVERSITY, Flagstaff, AZ   86001.
ARKANSAS POLYTECHIC COLLEGE, Russellville, AR   72801.
CALIFORNIA STATE POLYTECHNIC UNIVERSITY, Pomona, CA   91768.
CALIFORNIA STATE UNIVERSITY, Northridge, CA   91324.
CALIFORNIA STATE UNIVERSITY, Sacramento, CA   95819.
CALIFORNIA STATE UNIVERSITY, Chico, CA   95926.
UNIVERSITY OF CALIFORNIA, Davis, CA   95616.
UNIVERSITY OF SOUTHERN CALIFORNIA, Los Angeles, CA   90007.
HUMBOLDT STATE UNIVERSITY, Arcata, CA   95521.
COLORADO STATE UNIVERSITY, Fort Collins, CO   80521.
UNIVERSITY OF COLORADO, Boulder, CO   80302.
SOUTHERN CONNECTICUT STATE COLLEGE, New Haven, CT   06515.
YALE UNIVERSITY, New Haven, CT   06511.
UNIVERSITY OF FLORIDA, Gainesville, FL   32601.
UNIVERSITY OF GEORGIA, Athens, GA   30602.
UNIVERSITY OF IDAHO, Moscow, ID   83843.
SOUTHERN ILLINOIS UNIVERSITY, Carbondale, IL   67901.
BALL STATE UNIVERSITY, Muncie, IN   47306.
PURDUE UNIVERSITY, Lafayette, IN   47907.
IOWA STATE UNIVERSITY, Ames, IA   50010.
LOUISIANA STATE UNIVERSITY, Baton Rouge, LA   70803.
KANSAS STATE UNIVERSITY, Manhattan, KS   66506.

NORTHWESTERN STATE UNIVERSITY, Natchitoches, LA   71457.

UNIVERSITY OF MAINE, Orono, ME   04473.

NORTHEASTERN UNIVERSITY, Boston, MA   02115.

MICHIGAN STATE UNIVERSITY, East Lansing, MI   48824.

MICHIGAN TECHNOLOGICAL UNIVERSITY, Houghton, MI   49931.

UNIVERSITY OF MICHIGAN, Ann Arbor, MI   48104

UNIVERSITY OF MINNESOTA, Saint Paul, MN   55108.

UNIVERSITY OF SOUTHERN MISSISSIPPI, Hattiesburg, MS   39401.

UNIVERSITY OF MISSOURI, Columbia, MO   65201.

UNIVERSITY OF MONTANA, Missoula, MT   59801.

UNIVERSITY OF NEVADA, Reno, NV   89557.

STATE UNIVERSITY OF NEW YORK, COLLEGE OF ENVIRONMENTAL SCIENCE AND FORESTRY, Syracuse, NY   13210.

CORNELL UNIVERSITY, Ithaca, NY   14853.

NORTH CAROLINA STATE UNIVERSITY, Raleigh, NC   27607.

OHIO STATE UNIVERSITY, Columbus, OH   43210.

OREGON STATE UNIVERSITY, Corvallis, OR   97331.

UNIVERSITY OF OREGON, Eugene, OR   97403.

PENNSYLVANIA STATE UNIVERSITY, University Park, PA   16802.

SLIPPERY ROCK STATE COLLEGE, Slippery Rock, PA   16057.

CLEMSON UNIVERSITY, Clemson, SC   29631.

SOUTH DAKOTA STATE UNIVERSITY, Brookings, SD   57006.

UNIVERSITY OF TENNESSEE, Knoxville, TN   37916.

STEPHEN F. AUSTIN STATE UNIVERSITY, Nacogdoches, TX   75961.

TEXAS A & M UNIVERSITY, College Station, TX   77843.

UTAH STATE UNIVERSITY, Logan, UT   84322.

UNIVERSITY OF VERMONT, Burlington, VT   05401.

VIRGINIA POLYTECHNIC INSTITUTE AND STATE UNIVERSITY, Blacksburg, VA   24061.

UNIVERSITY OF WASHINGTON, Seattle, WA   98195.

WASHINGTON STATE UNIVERSITY, Pullman, WA   99163.

WEST VIRGINIA STATE UNIVERSITY, Morgantown, WV   26506.

UNIVERSITY OF WISCONSIN, Madison, WI   53706.

FORESTRY

The following colleges and universities offer instruction in forestry at the professional level.

AUBURN UNIVERSITY, DEPARTMENT OF FORESTRY, Auburn, AL   36830.

NORTHERN ARIZONA UNIVERSITY, SCHOOL OF FORESTRY, Flagstaff, AZ 86001.

UNIVERSITY OF ARIZONA, SCHOOL OF RENEWABLE NATURAL RESOURCES, Tucson, AZ   85721.

UNIVERSITY OF CALIFORNIA, DEPARTMENT OF FORESTRY AND RESOURCE MANAGEMENT, Berkeley, CA   94720.

COLORADO STATE UNIVERSITY, COLLEGE OF FORESTRY AND NATURAL RESOURCES, Fort Collins, CO   80523.

YALE UNIVERSITY, SCHOOL OF FORESTRY AND ENVIRONMENTAL STUDIES, New Haven, CT   06511.

UNIVERSITY OF FLORIDA, SCHOOL OF FOREST RESOURCES AND CONSERVATION, Gainesville, FL   32611.

UNIVERSITY OF GEORGIA, SCHOOL OF FOREST RESOURCES, Athens, GA 30601.

UNIVERSITY OF IDAHO, COLLEGE OF FORESTRY, WILDLIFE AND RANGE SCIENCES, Moscow, ID   83843.

UNIVERSITY OF ILLINOIS, DEPARTMENT OF FORESTRY, Urbana, IL   61801.

SOUTHERN ILLINOIS UNIVERSITY, DEPARTMENT OF FORESTRY, Carbondale, IL   62901.

PURDUE UNIVERSITY, DEPARTMENT OF FORESTRY AND NATURAL RESOURCES, Lafayette, IN   47907.

IOWA STATE UNIVERSITY, DEPARTMENT OF FORESTRY, Ames, IA   50011.

UNIVERSITY OF KENTUCKY, DEPARTMENT OF FORESTRY, Lexington, KY 40506.

LOUISIANA STATE UNIVERSITY, SCHOOL OF FORESTRY AND WILDLIFE MANAGEMENT, Baton Rouge, LA   70803.

UNIVERSITY OF MAINE, SCHOOL OF FOREST RESOURCES, Orono, ME 04473.

UNIVERSITY OF MASSACHUSETTS, DEPARTMENT OF FORESTRY AND WILDLIFE MANAGEMENT, Amherst, MA   01002.

MICHIGAN STATE UNIVERSITY, DEPARTMENT OF FORESTRY, East Lansing, MI   48823.

MICHIGAN TECHNOLOGICAL UNIVERSITY, SCHOOL OF FORESTRY AND WOOD PRODUCTS, Houghton, MI   49931.

UNIVERSITY OF MICHIGAN, SCHOOL OF NATURAL RESOURCES, Ann Arbor MI   48104.

UNIVERSITY OF MINNESOTA, COLLEGE OF FORESTRY, St. Paul, MN   55108.

MISSISSIPPI STATE UNIVERSITY, SCHOOL OF FOREST RESOURCES, Mississippi State, MS   39762.

University of Missouri, School of Forestry, Fisheries and Wildlife, Columbia, MO 65201.

University of Montana, School of Forestry, Missoula, MT 59801.

University of New Hampshire, Institute of Natural and Environmental Resources, Durham, NH 03824.

SUNY College of Environmental Science and Forestry, School of Environmental and Resource Management, Syracuse, NY 13210.

Duke University, School of Forestry and Environmental Studies, Durham, NC 27706.

North Carolina State University, School of Forest Resources, Raleigh, NC 27607.

Oklahoma State University, Department of Forestry, Stillwater, OK 74074.

Oregon State University, School of Forestry, Corvallis, OR 97331.

Pennsylvania State University, School of Forest Resources, University Park, PA 16802.

Clemson University, College of Forest and Recreation Resources, Clemson, SC 29631.

University of Tennessee, Department of Forestry, Knoxville, TN 37901.

Stephen F. Austin State University, School of Forestry, Nacogdoches, TX 75961.

Texas A&M University, Department of Forest Science, College Station, TX 77843.

Utah State University, College of Natural Resources, Logan, UT 84321.

University of Vermont, Department of Forestry, Burlington, VT 05401.

Virginia Polytechnic Institute and State University, Division of Forestry and Wildlife Resources, Blacksburg, VA 24061.

Washington State University, Department of Forestry and Range Management, Pullman, WA 99163.

University of Washington, College of Forest Resources, Seattle, WA 98195.

West Virginia University, Division of Forestry, Morgantown, WV 26506.

University of Wisconsin, Madison, Department of Forestry, Madison, WI 53706.

University of Wisconsin, Stevens Point, College of Natural Resources, Stevens Point, WI 54481.

AFFILIATED INSTITUTIONS

The following institutions offer professional forestry education and have met the standards for Society of American Foresters Affiliated Institutions:

UNIVERSITY OF ARKANSAS AT MONTICELLO, DEPARTMENT OF FORESTRY, Monticello, AR 71655.

HUMBOLDT STATE UNIVERSITY, SCHOOL OF NATURAL RESOURCES, Arcata, CA 95521.

CALIFORNIA POLYTECHNIC STATE UNIVERSITY, San Luis Obispo, CA 93401.

LOUISIANA TECH UNIVERSITY, SCHOOL OF FORESTRY, Ruston, LA 71270.

McNEESE STATE UNIVERSITY, DEPARTMENT OF AGRICULTURE, Lake Charles, LA 70601.

UNIVERSITY OF NEVADA, RENEWABLE NATURAL RESOURCES DIVISION, Reno, NV 89507.

RUTGERS UNIVERSITY, FORESTRY SECTION, COOK COLLEGE, New Brunswick, NJ 08903.

OHIO STATE UNIVERSITY, DIVISION-DEPARTMENT OF FORESTRY, Columbus, OH 43210.

OTHER INSTITUTIONS

These institutions offer professional forestry education.

WASHINGTON TECHNICAL INSTITUTE, DEPARTMENT OF FOREST MANAGEMENT, Washington, DC 20008.

UNIVERSITY OF THE SOUTH, DEPARTMENT OF FORESTRY, Sewanee, TN 37375.

PRE-PROFESSIONAL FORESTRY INSTITUTIONS

Many two-year and four-year institutions in the United States offer pre-professional forestry study programs which may qualify students for transfer to a professional forestry school at the sophomore or junior level. Often these do not include forestry courses, but lay a foundation for professional forestry education. Interested persons should contact the forestry school to which they wish to transfer for advice prior to enrolling for pre-professional forestry studies.

FRESHWATER RESOURCE MANAGEMENT

Universities offering bachelor degree granting curriculums in freshwater resource management:

UNIVERSITY OF ALASKA, Fairbanks, AK   99701.
UNIVERSITY OF ARIZONA, Tucson, AZ   85721.
AUBURN UNIVERSITY, Auburn, AL   36830.
CALIFORNIA POLYTECHNIC STATE UNIVERSITY, San Luis Obispo, CA   93401.
UNIVERSITY OF CALIFORNIA, Davis, CA   95616.
COLORADO STATE UNIVERSITY, Fort Collins, CO   80521.
CORNELL UNIVERSITY, Ithaca, New York, NY   14850.
EASTERN KENTUCKY UNIVERSITY, Richmond, KY   40475.
UNIVERSITY OF FLORIDA, Gainesville, FL   32601.
UNIVERSITY OF GEORGIA, Athens, GA   30601.
HUMBOLDT STATE UNIVERSITY, Arcata, CA   95521.
UNIVERSITY OF IDAHO, Moscow, ID   83843.
IOWA STATE UNIVERSITY, Ames, IA   50010.
LOUISIANA STATE UNIVERSITY, Baton Rouge, LA   70803.
UNIVERSITY OF MAINE, Orono, ME   04473.
UNIVERSITY OF MASSACHUSETTS, Amherst, MA   01002.
MICHIGAN STATE UNIVERSITY, East Lansing, MI   48823.
UNIVERSITY OF MICHIGAN, Ann Arbor, MI   48104.
UNIVERSITY OF MINNESOTA, St. Paul, MN   55108.
MISSISSIPPI STATE UNIVERSITY, Mississippi State, MS   39762.
UNIVERSITY OF MISSOURI, Columbia, MO   65201.
MONTANA STATE UNVERSITY, Bozeman, MT   59718.
NEW MEXICO STATE UNIVERSITY, Las Cruces, NM   88003.
OHIO STATE UNIVERSITY, Columbus, OH   43210.
OKLAHOMA STATE UNIVERSITY, Stillwater, OK   74074.
OREGON STATE UNIVERSITY, Corvallis, OR   97331.
SOUTH DAKOTA STATE UNIVERSITY, Brookings, SD   57006.
TENNESSEE TECHNOLOGICAL UNIVERSITY, Cookeville, TN   38501.

Texas A&M University, College Station, TX   77843.
Utah State University, Logan, UT   84321.
Virginia Polytechnic Institute and State University, Blacksburg, VA   24061.
University of Washington, Seattle, WA   98195.
University of Wisconsin, Stevens Point, WI   54481.

MARINE AND ESTUARINE RESOURCE MANAGEMENT

Universities offering graduate degree granting curricula in marine and estuarine resource management. This list includes only the major graduate programs offering six or more graduate courses in the marine sciences (marine fisheries, oceanography, marine biology, or other closely related subjects).

University of Alabama, Dauphin Island, AL   36528.
University of Alaska, Fairbanks, AK   99701.
University of Arizona, Tucson, AZ   85721.
California State University, Fullerton, CA   92634.
California State University, Long Beach, CA   90840.
California State University, Sacramento, CA   95819.
California State University, San Francisco, CA   94132.
California State University, San Luis Obispo, CA   93401.
Humboldt State University, Arcata, CA   95221.
San Francisco State University, CA   94132.
San Jose State University, CA   95100.
Stanford University, Pacific Grove, CA   93950.
University of California, Davis, CA   95616.
University of California, Los Angeles, CA   90024.
University of California, Santa Barbara, CA   93106.
University of California, Santa Cruz, CA   95060.
University of California, San Diego, CA   92037.
University of Southern California, Los Angeles, CA   90007.
University of the Pacific, Dillon Beach, CA   94929.
U.S. Coast Guard Academy, New London, CT   06320.
University of Connecticut, Storrs, CT   06268.
Yale University, New Haven, CT   06520.
University of Delaware, Newark, DE   19711.

THE AMERICAN UNIVERISTY, DC   20016.

THE CATHOLIC UNIVERSITY OF AMERICA, DC   20006.

FLORIDA ATLANTIC UNIVERSITY, Boca Raton, FL   33432.

FLORIDA INSTITUTE OF TECHNOLOGY, Melbourne, FL   32902.

FLORIDA STATE UNIVERSITY, Tallahassee, FL   32306.

UNIVERSITY OF FLORIDA, Gainesville, FL   32601.

UNIVERSITY OF MIAMI, FL   33149.

UNIVERSITY OF SOUTH FLORIDA, St. Petersburg, FL   33701.

UNIVERSITY OF WEST FLORIDA, Pensacola, FL   32504.

GEORGIA INSTITUTE OF TECHNOLOGY, Atlanta, GA   30332.

UNIVERSITY OF GEORGIA, Athens, GA   30602.

UNIVERSITY OF HAWAII, Honolulu, HI   96822.

UNIVERSITY OF CHICAGO, IL   60637.

LOUISIANA STATE UNIVERSITY, Baton Rouge, LA   70803.

UNIVERSITY OF MAINE, Orono, ME   04473.

JOHNS HOPKINS UNIVERSITY, Baltimore, MD   21218.

UNIVERSITY OF MARYLAND, College Park, MD   20742.

BOSTON UNIVERSITY, Woods Hole, MA   02543.

HARVARD UNIVERSITY, Cambridge, MA   02138.

MASSACHUSETTS INSTITUTE OF TECHNOLOGY, Cambridge, MA   02139.

NORTHEASTERN UNIVERSITY, Boston, MA   02115.

UNIVERSITY OF MASSACHUSETTS, Amherst, MA   01002.

UNIVERSITY OF MICHIGAN, Ann Arbor, MI   48104.

UNIVERSITY OF MISSISSIPPI, Oxford, MS   38677.

MISSISSIPPI STATE UNIVERSITY, Mississippi State, MS   39762.

UNIVERSITY OF SOUTHERN MISSISSIPPI, Hattiesburg, MS   39401.

SOUTHWEST MISSOURI STATE UNIVERSITY, Springfield, MO   65802.

UNIVERSITY OF NEW HAMPSHIRE, Durham, NH   03824.

FAIRLEIGH DICKENSON UNIVERSITY, Madison, NJ   07940.

RUTGERS UNIVERSITY, New Brunswick, NJ   08903.

STEVENS INSTITUTE OF TECHNOLOGY, Hoboken, NJ   07030.

ADELPHI UNIVERSITY, Garden City, Long Island, NY   11530.

C. W. POST OF LONG ISLAND UNIVERSITY, Greenvale, NY   11548.

CITY UNIVERSITY OF NEW YORK, NY   10031.

COLUMBIA UNIVERSITY, NY   10027.

CORNELL UNIVERSITY, Ithaca, NY   14853.

ST. JOHN'S UNIVERSITY, Jamaica, NY   11432.

STATE UNIVERSITY OF NEW YORK, Stony Brook, NY   11794.

STATE UNIVERSITY OF NEW YORK MARITIME COLLEGE, Bronx, NY 10465.

DUKE UNIVERSITY, Durham, NC 27706.

EAST CAROLINA UNIVERSITY, Greenville, NC 27834.

NORTH CAROLINA STATE UNIVERSITY, Raleigh, NC 27607.

UNIVERSITY OF NORTH CAROLINA, Chapel Hill, NC 27514.

OREGON STATE UNIVERSITY, Corvallis, OR 97331.

UNIVERSITY OF OREGON, Eugene, OR 97403.

LEHIGH UNIVERSITY, Bethlehem, PA 18015.

UNIVERSITY OF RHODE ISLAND, Kingston, RI 02881.

CLEMSON UNIVERSITY, Clemson, SC 29631.

UNIVERSITY OF SOUTH CAROLINA, Columbia, SC 29208.

TEXAS A&M UNIVERSITY, College Station, TX 77843.

UNIVERSITY OF HOUSTON, TX 77004.

UNIVERSITY OF TEXAS, Austin, TX 78712.

COLLEGE OF WILLIAM AND MARY, Gloucester Point, VA 23062.

OLD DOMINION UNIVERSITY, Norfolk, VA 23508.

UNIVERSITY OF VIRGINIA, Gloucester Point, VA 23062.

UNIVERSITY OF WASHINGTON, Seattle, WA 98195.

UNIVERSITY OF WISCONSIN, Madison, WI 53706.

RANGE MANAGEMENT

Names and addresses of schools in the United States belonging to the Range Science Education Council:

COLLEGE OF BIOLOGICAL SCIENCES & RENEWABLE RESOURCES, UNIVERSITY OF ALASKA, College, AK 99735.

SCHOOL OF RENEWABLE NATURAL RESOURCES, UNIVERSITY OF ARIZONA, Tucson, AZ 85721.

DIVISION OF AGRICULTURE, ARIZONA STATE UNIVERSITY, Tempe, AZ 85281.

DEPARTMENT OF BOTANY & RANGE SCIENCE, BRIGHAM YOUNG UNIVERSITY, Provo, UT 85601.

DEPARTMENT OF FORESTRY & CONSERVATION, UNIVERSITY OF CALIFORNIA, Berkeley, CA 94720.

DEPARTMENT OF AGRONOMY & RANGE SCIENCE, UNIVERSITY OF CALIFORNIA, Davis, CA 95616.

ANIMAL SCIENCE DEPARTMENT, CALIFORNIA POLYTECHNIC STATE UNIVERSITY, San Luis Obispo, CA   93401.

DEPARTMENT OF PLANT & SOIL SCIENCES, CALIFORNIA STATE UNIVERSITY CHICO, Chico, CA   95925.

RANGE SCIENCE DEPARTMENT, COLLEGE OF FORESTRY & NATURAL RESOURCES, COLORADO STATE UNIVERSITY, Fort Collins, CO   80523.

SCHOOL OF FOREST RESOURCES AND CONSERVATION, UNIVERSITY OF FLORIDA, Gainesville, FL   32601.

DEPARTMENT OF BIOLOGICAL SCIENCES, FORT HAYS STATE UNIVERSITY, Hays, KS   67601.

DEPARTMENT OF RANGE MANAGEMENT, SCHOOL OF NATURAL RESOURCES, HUMBOLDT STATE UNIVERSITY, Arcata, CA   95521.

COLLEGE OF FORESTRY, WILDLIFE & RANGE SCIENCE, UNIVERSITY OF IDAHO, Moscow, ID   83843.

DEPARTMENT OF FORESTRY, IOWA STATE UNIVERSITY, Ames, IA   50010.

DEPARTMENT OF AGRONOMY, KANSAS STATE UNIVERSITY, Manhattan, KS 66502.

SCHOOL OF FORESTRY, UNIVERSITY OF MONTANA, Missoula, MT   59801.

DEPARTMENT OF ANIMAL & RANGE SCIENCES, MONTANA STATE UNIVERSITY, Bozeman, MT   59715.

DEPARTMENT OF AGRONOMY, COLLEGE OF AGRICULTURE, UNIVERSITY OF NEBRASKA, Lincoln, NE   68503.

DIVISION OF RENEWABLE NATURAL RESOURCES, RENEWABLE RESOURCES CENTER, UNIVERSITY OF NEVADA, RENO, NV   89502.

DEPARTMENT OF ANIMAL, RANGE AND WILDLIFE SCIENCES, NEW MEXICO STATE UNIVERSITY, Las Cruces, NM   88003.

SCHOOL OF FORESTRY, NORTHERN ARIZONA UNIVERSITY, Flagstaff, AZ 86001.

DEPARTMENT OF BOTANY, NORTH DAKOTA STATE UNIVERSITY, Fargo, ND 48102.

DEPARTMENT OF AGRONOMY, OKLAHOMA STATE UNIVERSITY, Stillwater, OK   74074.

RANGELAND RESOURCES, OREGON STATE UNIVERSITY, Corvallis, OR 97331.

ANIMAL SCIENCE DEPARTMENT, SOUTH DAKOTA STATE UNIVERSITY, Brookings, SD   57006.

RANGE ANIMAL SCIENCE DEPARTMENT, SUL ROSS STATE UNIVERSITY, Alpine, TX   79830.

COLLEGE OF AGRICULTURE, TEXAS A&I UNIVERSITY IN KINGSVILLE, Kingsville, TX   78363.

DEPARTMENT OF RANGE SCIENCE, TEXAS A&M UNIVERSITY, College Station, TX 77843.

DEPARTMENT OF RANGE & WILDLIFE MANAGEMENT, TEXAS TECH UNIVERSITY, Lubbock, TX 79409.

RANGE SCIENCE DEPARTMENT, COLLEGE OF NATURAL RESOURCES, UTAH STATE UNIVERSITY, Logan, UT 84321.

COLLEGE OF FOREST RESOURCES, UNIVERSITY OF WASHINGTON, Seattle, WA 98105.

DEPARTMENT OF FORESTRY & RANGE MANAGEMENT, WASHINGTON STATE UNIVERSITY, Pullman, WA 99163.

RANGE MANAGEMENT SECTION, PLANT SCIENCE DIVISION, UNIVERSITY OF WYOMING, University Station, Box 3354, Laramie, WY 82070.

WATERSHED MANAGEMENT

Colleges and universities offering professional or degree granting curriculums with majors or options in the field of watershed management.

UNIVERSITY OF ARIZONA, Tucson, AZ 85721.

UNIVERSITY OF CALIFORNIA, Berkeley, CA 94720.

COLORADO STATE UNIVERSITY, Fort Collins, CO 80523.

UNIVERSITY OF GEORGIA, Athens, GA 30601.

UNIVERSITY OF IDAHO, Moscow, ID 84843.

UNIVERSITY OF MINNESOTA, St. Paul, MN 55108.

UNIVERSITY OF MISSOURI, Columbia, MO 65201.

UNIVERSITY OF NEVADA, Reno, NV 89507.

OREGON STATE UNIVERSITY, Corvallis, OR 97331.

PENNSYLVANIA STATE UNIVERSITY, University Park, PA 16802.

SCHOOL OF ENVIRONMENTAL AND RESOURCE MANAGEMENT, STATE UNIVERSITY OF NEW YORK, Syracuse, NY 65201.

UTAH STATE UNIVERSITY, Logan, UT 84321.

WASHINGTON STATE UNIVERSITY, Pullman, WA 99163.

UNIVERSITY OF WASHINGTON, Seattle, WA 98195.

WEST VIRGINIA UNIVERSITY, Morgantown, WV 20506.

YALE UNIVERSITY, New Haven, CT 06511.

WILDLIFE BIOLOGY AND MANAGEMENT

Colleges and universities in the United States offering major programs in wildlife biology and management.

UNIVERSITY OF ALASKA, Fairbanks, AK 99701.
UNIVERSITY OF ARIZONA, Tucson, AZ 85721.
ARIZONA STATE UNIVERSITY, Tempe, AZ 85281.
ARKANSAS POLYTECHNIC UNIVERSITY, Russellville, AR 72801.
AUBURN UNIVERSITY, Auburn, AL 36830.
UNIVERSITY OF CALIFORNIA, Berkeley, CA 94720.
UNIVERSITY OF CALIFORNIA, Davis, CA 95616.
HUMBOLDT STATE UNIVERSITY, Arcata, CA 95521.
SAN JOSE STATE UNIVERSITY, San Jose, CA 95192.
CLEMSON UNIVERSITY, Clemson, SC 29631.
COLORADO STATE UNIVERSITY, Fort Collins, CO 80521.
UNIVERSITY OF CONNECTICUT, Storrs, CT 06268.
CORNELL UNIVERSITY, Ithaca, NY 14850.
UNIVERSITY OF FLORIDA, Gainesville, FL 32601.
FROSTBURG STATE COLLEGE, Frostburg, MD 21532.
UNIVERSITY OF GEORGIA, Athens, GA 30602.
UNIVERSITY OF IDAHO, Moscow, ID 83843.
IDAHO STATE UNIVERSITY, Pocatello, ID 83209.
UNIVERSITY OF ILLINOIS, Urbana, IL 61801.
SOUTHERN ILLINOIS UNIVERSITY, Carbondale, IL 62901.
IOWA STATE UNIVERSITY, Ames, IA 50011.
KANSAS STATE UNIVERSITY, Manhattan, KS 66506.
EASTERN KENTUCKY UNIVERSITY, Richmond, KY 40475.
LOUISIANA STATE UNIVERSITY, Baton Rouge, LA 70803.
LOUISIANA TECH UNIVERSITY, Ruston, LA 71270.
NORTHEAST LOUISIANA UNIVERSITY, Monroe, LA 71201.
NORTHWESTERN STATE UNIVERSITY, Natchitoches, LA 71457.
UNIVERSITY OF MAINE, Orono, ME 04473.
UNIVERSITY OF MASSACHUSETTS, Amherst, MA 01002.
UNIVERSITY OF MICHIGAN, Ann Arbor, MI 48104.
MICHIGAN STATE UNIVERSITY, East Lansing, MI 48824.
UNIVERSITY OF MINNESOTA, St. Paul, MN 55108.
MISSISSIPPI STATE UNIVERSITY, State College, MS 39762.
UNIVERSITY OF MISSOURI, Columbia, MO 65201.
UNIVERSITY OF MONTANA, Missoula, MT 59812.
MONTANA STATE UNIVERSITY, Bozeman, MT 59715.
MURRAY STATE UNIVERSITY, Murray, KY 42071.
UNIVERSITY OF NEBRASKA, Lincoln, NE 68503.

UNIVERSITY OF NEW HAMPSHIRE, Durham, NH   03824.

NEW MEXICO STATE UNIVERSITY, Las Cruces, NM   88003.

STATE UNIVERSITY OF NEW YORK, Syracuse, NY   13210.

NORTH CAROLINA STATE UNIVERSITY, Raleigh, NC   27607.

UNIVERSITY OF NORTH DAKOTA, Grand Forks, ND   58201.

NORTH DAKOTA STATE UNIVERSITY, Fargo, ND   58102.

OHIO STATE UNIVERSITY, Columbus, OH   43210.

OKLAHOMA STATE UNIVERSITY, Stillwater, OK   74074.

SOUTHEASTERN OKLAHOMA STATE UNIVERSITY, Durant, OK   74701.

OREGON STATE UNIVERSITY, Corvallis, OR   97331.

PENNSYLVANIA STATE UNIVERSITY, University Park, PA   16802.

PURDUE UNIVERSITY, Lafayette, IN   47907.

UNIVERSITY OF RHODE ISLAND, Kingston, RI   02881.

RUTGERS UNIVERSITY, New Brunswick, NJ   08903.

SOUTH DAKOTA STATE UNIVERSITY, Brookings, SD   57006.

UNIVERSITY OF TENNESSEE, Knoxville, TN   37901.

TENNESSEE TECH UNIVERSITY, Cookeville, TN   38501.

TEXAS A & M UNIVERSITY, College Station, TX   77843.

TEXAS TECH UNIVERSITY, Lubbock, TX   79409.

UTAH STATE UNIVERSITY, Logan, UT   84322.

VIRGINIA POLYTECHNIC INSTITUTE & STATE UNIVERSITY, Blacksburg, VA   24061.

UNIVERSITY OF WASHINGTON, Seattle, WA   98195.

WASHINGTON STATE UNIVERSITY, Pullman, WA   99163.

WEST VIRGINIA UNIVERSITY, Morgantown, WV   26506.

UNIVERSITY OF WISCONSIN, Madison, WI   53706.

UNIVERSITY OF WISCONSIN, Stevens Point, WI   54481.

UNIVERSITY OF WYOMING, Laramie, WY   82070.

BIOLOGY

A bachelor's degree is the minimum academic qualification for the professional biologist. This basic degree can be obtained at most of the hundreds of universities and colleges in America. For the undergraduate student, any accredited institution should provide a suitable curriculum.

LAND USE

Land use cannot be clearly identified as a particular profession from an academic standpoint. There are few academic curriculums that use a land use title. The reason is because land use is a broad and general term which in application draws on a wide range of academic disciplines. Basically, a broad education is needed. Institutions are not named since they vary widely in organization, educational emphasis content, direction, and character of advanced courses.

Appendix B

Some publications that provide further information on careers in natural resources management are listed below.

America's Natural Resources. (2nd ed). Edited by Charles H. Callison. Ronald Press Co., New York, NY. 1967.

Careers in Natural Resource Conservation. By Fred W. Herbert. Henry Z. Walck, Inc., New York, NY. 1965.

Career Opportunities: Ecology, Conservation & Environmental Control. J. G. Ferguson Editorial Staff. Doubleday and Co., Garden City, NY. 1971.

Conservation of Natural Resources. (4th ed.) By Guy-Harold Smith. John Wiley & Sons, New York, NY. 1971.

Making a Living in Conservation: A Guide to Outdoor Careers. By Albert M. Day. Stackpole, Harrisburg, PA. 1971.

Natural Resources Conservation: An Ecological Approach. (2nd ed.) By Oliver S. Owen. Macmillan Co., New York, NY. 1975.

Origins of American Conservation. Edited by Henry Clepper. Ronald Press Co., New York, NY. 1966.

Our Natural Resources. (4th ed.) By Harry B. Kircher and P. E. McNall. Interstate Printers and Publishers, Danville, IL. 1976.

Renewable Resources for Industrial Materials. Board of Agriculture and Renewable Resources, National Research Council/National Academy of Sciences, Washington, DC. 1976.

ENVIRONMENTAL CONSERVATION

Books for further reading in environmental conservation.

An Introduction to Environmental Sciences. By Joseph M. Moran,

Michael D. Morgan, James H. Wiersma. Little Brown and Co., Boston, MA. 1973.

Ecology and the Quality of our Environment. (2nd ed.) By Charles H. Southwick, D. Van Nostrand Co., New York, NY. 1976.

Energy, Ecology, Economy. By Gerald Garvey. W. W. Norton & Co., Inc., New York, NY. 1972.

Environmental Conservation. (3rd ed.) By Raymond F. Dasmann. John Wiley and Sons, Inc., New York, NY. 1972.

Man and the Environment. By Arthur S. Boughey. Macmillan Co., New York, NY. 1971.

TANSTAAFL. By Edwin G. Dolan. Holt, Rinehart, and Winston, Inc., New York, NY. 1971.

The Environmental Handbook. Edited by Garrett De Bell. Ballantine Books, Inc., New York, NY. 1970.

SOIL CONSERVATION

Publications providing further information about careers in soil conservation.

A Soil Science Career for You in SCS. Soil Conservation Service, U.S. Department of Agriculture, Washington, DC. 1971.

An Engineering Career for You in the Soil Conservation Service. Soil Conservation Service, U.S. Department of Agriculture, Washington, DC. 1975.

Careers for the 70's—Conservation. By Ed Dodd. Crowell-Collier Press, New York, NY. 1971.

Careers in Conservation. Soil Conservation Society of America, Ankeny, IA. (Pamphlet.)

Encyclopedia of Careers and Vocational Guidance. Edited by William Hopke. J. G. Ferguson Co., Chicago, IL. 1975.

Guide to Conservation Careers. National Association of Conservation Districts, League City, TX. 1977. (Pamphlet.)

Opportunities in Environmental Careers. By Odom Fanning. Vocational Guidance Manuals, Inc., Louisville, KY. 1976.

Students: Start Your Career in SCS Before You Graduate. Soil Conservation Service, U.S. Department of Agriculture, Washington, DC. 1971.

Journal of Soil and Water Conservation provides much current information about work and progress in this field. It is published by Soil Conservation Society of America, Ankeny, IA.

OUTDOOR RECREATION

The following books provide further information about the field of outdoor recreation.

Elements of Outdoor Recreation Planning. Edited by B. L. Driver. University of Michigan Press, Ann Arbor, MI. 1974.

Elements of Park and Recreation Administration. (3rd ed.) By Charles E. Doell and Louis F. Twardzik. Burgess Publishing Co., Minneapolis, MN. 1973.

Forest Recreation. (2nd ed.) Robert W. Douglas. Pergamon Press, Inc., New York, NY. 1975.

Interpretation of Historic Sites. By William Anderson and Shirley Low. American Association for State and Local History, Nashville, TN. 1976.

Interpreting the Environment. Edited by Grant W. Sharpe. John Wiley and Sons, Inc., New York, NY. 1976.

Outdoor Recreation: Forest, Park, and Wilderness. By Joseph R. McCall and Virginia N. McCall. Benziger, Bruce and Glencoe, Inc., (Macmillan Publishing Co.), Riverside, NJ. 1977.

Outdoor Recreation in America. By Clayne R. Jensen. Burgess Publishing Co., Minneapolis, MN. 1970.

Outdoor Recreation Planning. By Allen Jubenville. W. B. Saunders Co., Philadelphia, PA. 1976.

Problem Solving in Recreation and Parks. By Joseph J. Bannon. Prentice-Hall, Inc., Englewood Cliffs, NJ. 1972.

Recreational Use of Wild Lands. (2nd ed.) By C. Frank Brockman and Lawrence C. Merriam, Jr. McGraw-Hill Book Co., New York, NY. 1973.

The National Park Service. By William C. Everhart. Frederick A. Praeger, Inc., New York, NY. 1972.

Wilderness and the American Mind. By Roderick Nash. Yale University Press, New Haven, CT. 1967.

Journals and Other Publications

American Forests. American Forestry Association, Washington, D.C.

Journal of Forestry. Society of American Foresters, Washington, D.C.

The Interpreter. Received through membership in Western Interpreters Association. La Jolla, CA.

Journal of Interpretation. Received through membership in Association of Interpretive Naturalists. Derwood, MD.

Parks and Recreation Magazine. National Recreation and Park Association, Arlington, VA.

FORESTRY

Publications that provide background information on forestry.

American Forests magazine, published by The American Forestry Association, Washington, DC.

Forest Service Career Guide. Forest Service, U.S. Department of Agriculture, Washington, DC. 1974.

Forestry and Its Career Opportunities. (3rd ed.) By Hardy L. Shirley. McGraw-Hill Book Co., New York, NY. 1973.

Introduction to American Forestry. (4th ed.) By Grant W. Sharpe, John C. Hendee, and Shirley W. Allen. McGraw-Hill Book Co., New York, NY. 1976.

Journal of Forestry, published by the Society of American Foresters, Washington, DC.

Making a Living in Conservation. By Albert M. Day. Stackpole Co., Harrisburg, PA. 1971.

Opportunities in Forestry Careers. By E. L. Demmon. Data Courier, Inc., Louisville, KY. 1975.

Your Future in Forestry. By David H. Hanaburgh. Arco Publishing Co., New York, N.Y. 1970.

What the Forest Service Does. Forest Service, U.S. Department of Agriculture, Washington, DC. 1974.

FRESHWATER RESOURCE MANAGEMENT

Publications for further reading about fisheries biology and science as a profession.

A Century of Fisheries in North America. Edited by Norman G. Benson, American Fisheries Society, Washington, DC. 1970.

Fisheries. A bulletin of the American Fisheries Society (bimonthly), Bethesda, MD.

Freshwater Fishery Biology. By Karl F. Lagler. W. C. Brown, Dubuque, IA. 1956.

Growth and Ecology of Fish Populations. By A. H. Weatherley. Academic Press, New York, NY. 1972.

Inland Fisheries Management. By Alex Calhoun. California Department of Fish and Game, Sacramento, CA. 1966.

Introductory Fisheries Science. By Robert T. Lackey. Sea Grant Program, Virginia Polytechnic Institute and State University, Blacksburg, VA. 1974.

Introduction to the Fishery Sciences. By William A. Royce. Academic Press, New York, NY. 1972.

Principles of Fishery Science. By W. Harry Everhart, Alfred W. Eipper, and William D. Youngs. Cornell University Press, Ithaca, NY. 1975.

Reservoir Fisheries and Limnology. Edited by Gordon E. Hall. American Fisheries Society, Washington, DC. 1971.

Sport Fishing USA. By Dan Saults and Michael Walker. U.S. Department of the Interior, Washington, DC. 1971.

Transactions of the American Fisheries Society. (Quarterly.) Bethesda, MD.

MARINE AND ESTUARINE RESOURCE MANAGEMENT

Publications providing additional information on marine and estuarine resources.

A Symposium on Estuarine Fisheries. Edited by R. F. Smith, A. H. Swartz, and W. H. Massman. American Fisheries Society, Washington, DC. 1966.

Coastal Resource Management. By R. B. Ditton, J. L. Seymour, and G. C. Swanson. Lexington Books, Lexington, MA. 1977.

Ecology, Utilization, and Management of Marine Fisheries. By G. A. Rounsefell. C. V. Mosby Co., St. Louis, MO. 1975.

Fisheries as a Profession, A Career Guide for the Field of Fisheries Science. American Fisheries Society, Bethesda, MD. 1976.

Fisheries Resources of the Sea and Their Management. By D. H. Cushing. Oxford University Press, New York. 1975.

Opportunities in Oceanography. (4th ed.) Smithsonian Institution Press, Washington, DC. 1971.

Principles of Fishery Science. By W. A. Everhart, A. W. Eipper, and W. D. Youngs. Cornell University Press, Ithaca, NY. 1975.

The Management of Marine Fisheries. By J. A. Gulland. University of Washington Press, Seattle, WA. 1974.

The Oceans and You. Marine Technology Society, Washington, DC. 1973.

Your Career in Oceanography. By W. T. Boyd. N. J. Messner Publishers, New York, NY. 1968.

Your Future in Oceanography. By N. H. Gaber. R. Roser Press, New York, NY. 1967.

The following journals also provide periodical information on marine and estuarine management and resources.

Fisheries and *Transactions,* published by American Fisheries Society, Bethesda, MD.

Fishery Bulletin and *Marine Fisheries Review,* published by National Marine Fisheries Service, U.S. Department of Commerce, Washington, DC.

Limnology and Oceanography, published by American Society of Limnology and Oceanography, University of Washington, Seattle, WA.

RANGE MANAGEMENT

Publications dealing with range management.

Journal of Range Management, published bimonthly by the Society for Range Management, Denver, CO.

Range Management. By L. A. Stoddart et al. McGraw-Hill Book Co., New York, NY. 1975.

Rangeland Management. By Harold F. Heady. McGraw-Hill Book Co., New York, NY. 1975.

Rangeland Management for Livestock Production. By Hershel M. Bell. University of Oklahoma Press, Norman, OK. 1973.

Rangeman's Journal, published bimonthly by the Society for Range Management, Denver, CO.

WATERSHED MANAGEMENT

The following publications provide information on the conservation and management of water resources.

An Outline of Forest Hydrology. By John D. Hewlett and Wade L. Nutter. University of Georgia Press, Athens, GA. 1969.

Career Opportunities in Water Resources. Universities Council on Water Resources, University of Nebraska, Lincoln, NE.

Guidelines for Watershed Management. Edited by Samuel H. Kunkle and John L. Thames. Food and Agriculture Organization of the United Nations, Rome, Italy. 1977.

Journal of Soil and Water Conservation, published by the Soil Conservation Society of America, Ankeny, IA.

Proceedings of International Symposium on Forest Hydrology. Edited by William E. Sopper and Howard W. Lull. Pergamon Press, New York, NY. 1967.

Water Resources Bulletin. St. Anthony Falls Hydraulic Laboratory, Minneapolis, MN.

Wildland Watershed Management. By Donald R. Satterlund. Ronald Press Co., New York, NY. 1972.

WILDLIFE BIOLOGY AND MANAGEMENT

Publications dealing with wildlife biology and management.

A Manual of Wildlife Conservation. Edited by R. D. Teague. The Wildlife Society, Washington, DC. 1971.

Compensation in the Fields of Fish and Wildlife Management. National Wildlife Federation, Washington, DC. 1977.

Environmental Conservation. By R. F. Dasmann. (3rd ed.) John Wiley & Sons, New York, NY. 1972.

Game Management. By Aldo Leopold. Chas. Scribner's Sons, New York, NY. 1933.

Natural Resources and Public Relations. By D. L. Gilbert (2nd ed.) The Wildlife Society, Washington, DC. 1975.

Opportunities in Environmental Careers. By Odom Fanning. Vocational Guidance Manuals, University Publishing and Distributing Corporation, New York, NY. 1971.

Placing American Wildlife Management in Perspective. Wildlife Management Institute, Washington, DC. 1974.

Readings in Wildlife Conservation. Edited by J. A. Bailey et al. The Wildlife Society, Washington, DC. 1975.

Wildlife Legacy. By Durward L. Allen. (Rev.) Funk & Wagnall's, New York, NY. 1962.

Wildlife Management, I and II. By Rueben E. Trippensee. McGraw-Hill Book Co., New York, NY. 1949 and 1953.

Wildlife Management and Conservation. By James B. Trefethen. D. C. Heath & Co., Boston, MA. 1964.

Wildlife Management Techniques. Edited by S. H. Schemnitz. (4th ed.) The Wildlife Society, Washington, DC. 1978.

BIOLOGY

Some publications that give background information on biology as a science and a career.

An Introduction to Biology. By Robert M. Chute. Harper and Row, New York, NY. 1976.

Biology—A Functional Approach. By M. B. V. Roberts. Ronald Press Co., New York, NY. 1972.

Biology and Society. By P. R. Ehrlich et al. McGraw-Hill Book Co., New York, NY. 1976.

Biology in the World of the Future. By Hal Hellman. M. Evans & Co. (Lippincott Co.), Philadelphia, PA. 1971.

Biology Made Simple. By Ethel R. Hanauer. Doubleday & Co., Garden City, NY. 1972.

BioScience, a periodical journal published by the American Institute of Biological Sciences, Arlington, VA.

Invitation to Biology. By Helene Curtis. Worth Publishers, New York, NY. 1975.

The Living Earth: An Introduction to Biology. By Uldis Roze. T. Y. Crowell Co., New York, NY. 1976.

This Is Our World. By Paul B. Sears. University of Oklahoma Press, Norman, OK. 1971.

Introductory Biology. By K. C. Jones and A. J. Gaudin. John Wiley & Sons, New York, NY. 1977.

LAND USE

Some land use references follow.

Coastal Zone Management: Multiple Use with Conservation. Edited by J. S. Peel Brahtz. John Wiley and Sons, New York, NY. 1972.

Council on Environmental Quality. First Annual Report. U.S. Government Printing Office, Washington, DC. 1970.

Land Use. By Kenneth P. Davis. McGraw-Hill Book Co., New York, NY. 1976.

Land Use in the United States: Exploitation or Conservation. Edited by Grant S. McClellan. W. H. Wilson Co., New York, NY. 1971.

Land Use Planning and Zoning. By J. R. Dilworth. School of Forestry, Oregon State University, Corvallis, OR. 1971.

The Politics of Conservation. By F. D. Smith. Pantheon Books, Random House, New York, NY. 1966.

The Use of Land: A Citizen's Policy Guide to Urban Growth. Task Force Report sponsored by Rockefeller Brothers Fund, New York, NY. 1973.

Appendix C

ORGANIZATIONS

This is a list of professional and scientific societies, citizens and trade associations, and similar organizations concerned with natural resources, particularly their conservation and management.

Conservation Directory is published annually by the National Wildlife Federation, 1412–16th Street, NW, Washington, DC 20036. It provides a comprehensive list of organizations, agencies, and officials concerned with natural resource use and management.

GENERAL

AMERICAN CONSERVATION ASSOCIATION, INC., 30 Rockefeller Plaza, Room 5425, New York, NY   10020.

AMERICAN INSTITUTE OF BIOLOGICAL SCIENCES, INC., 1401 Wilson Boulevard, Arlington, VA   22209.

ASSOCIATION OF INTERPRETIVE NATURALISTS, INC., 6700 Needwood Road, Derwood, MD   20855.

BOY SCOUTS OF AMERICA, North Brunswick, NJ   08902.

CAMP FIRE GIRLS, INC., 4601 Madison Avenue, Kansas City, MO 64112.

THE CONSERVATION FOUNDATION, 1717 Massachusetts Avenue, NW, Washington, DC   20036.

ECOLOGICAL SOCIETY OF AMERICA, C/o The Ecosystem Center, Marine Biological Laboratory, Woods Hole, MA   02543.

FRIENDS OF THE EARTH, 124 Spear Street, San Francisco, CA   94105.

GIRL SCOUTS OF THE UNITED STATES OF AMERICA, 830 Third Avenue, New York, NY   10022.

IZAAK WALTON LEAGUE OF AMERICA, INC., 1800 North Kent Street, Arlington, VA   22209.

LEAGUE OF WOMEN VOTERS OF THE UNITED STATES, 1730 M Street, NW, Washington, DC   20036.

NATIONAL AUDUBON SOCIETY, 950 Third Street, New York, NY   10022.

NATURAL RESOURCES COUNCIL OF AMERICA, P. O. Box 20, Tracys Landing, MD   20869.

THE NATURE CONSERVANCY, Suite 800, 1800 North Kent Street, Arlington, VA   22209.

RESOURCES FOR THE FUTURE, 1755 Massachusetts Avenue, NW, Washington, DC   20036.

SIERRA CLUB, 530 Bush Street, San Francisco, CA   94108.

THE WILDERNESS SOCIETY, 1901 Pennsylvania Avenue, NW, Washington, DC   20006.

ENVIRONMENTAL CONSERVATION

AMERICAN CONSERVATION ASSOCIATION, INC., 30 Rockefeller Plaza, New York, NY   10020.

ASPEN INSTITUTE PROGRAM IN ENVIRONMENT & QUALITY OF LIFE, 1755 Massachusetts Ave. NW, Washington, DC   20036.

BOLTON INSTITUTE, THE, 1835 K St. NW, Washington, DC   20006.

CONSERVATION FOUNDATION, THE, 1717 Massachusetts Ave., NW, Washington, DC   20036.

COUNCIL ON POPULATION AND ENVIRONMENT, INC., 53 Jackson Blvd., Chicago, IL   60604.

ENVIRONMENTAL ACTION FOUNDATION, INC., 724 Dupont Circle Bldg., Washington, DC   20036.

ENVIRONMENTAL ACTION, INC., 1346 Connecticut Ave., NW, Washington, DC   20036.

ENVIRONMENTAL DEFENSE FUND, INC., 475 Park Avenue South, New York, NY   10016.

ENVIRONMENTAL POLICY CENTER, 317 Pennsylvania Ave., SE, Washington, DC   20003.

ENVIRONMENTAL RESEARCH INSTITUTE, Box 156, Moose, WY   83012.

FRIENDS OF THE EARTH, 124 Spear St., San Francisco, CA   94105.

GARDEN CLUB OF AMERICA, THE, 598 Madison Ave., New York, NY   10022.

INTERNATIONAL INSTITUTE FOR ENVIRONMENT AND DEVELOPMENT, 1302 18th St., NW, Washington, DC   20036.

Izaak Walton League of America, The, 1800 North Kent St., Arlington, VA   22209.

National Association for Environmental Education, P. O. Box 560931, Miami, FL   33156.

National Audubon Society, 950 Third Ave., New York, NY   10022.

Natural Resources Defense Council, Inc., 122 East 42nd St., New York, NY   10017.

Natural Resources Council of America, P. O. Box 20, Tracys Landing, MD   20869.

Sierra Club, 530 Bush St., San Francisco, CA   94108.

Student Conservation Association, Inc., Box 550, Charlestown, NH 03603.

SOIL CONSERVATION

American Association of Nurserymen, 935 Southern Building, Washington, DC   20005.

American Forestry Association, 1319 18th Street, NW, Washington, DC   20036.

American Institute of Planners, 1776 Massachusetts Avenue, NW, Washington, DC   20036.

American Society for Range Management, 2120 S. Birch Street, Denver, CO   80222.

American Society of Agricultural Engineers, P.O. Box 229, St. Joseph, MI   49085.

American Society of Agronomy, 677 S. Segoe Road, Madison, WI 53711.

Future Farmers of America, P.O. Box 15160, Alexandria, VA   22309.

National Association of Conservation Districts, 1025 Vermont Avenue, NW, Washington, DC   20005.

Resources for the Future, Inc., 1755 Massachusetts Avenue, NW, Washington, DC   20036.

Society of American Foresters, 5400 Grosvenor Lane, Washington, DC   20014.

Soil Conservation Society of America, 7515 N.E. Ankeny Road, Ankeny, IA   50021.

Urban Land Institute, 1200 18th Street, NW, Washington, DC 20036.

OUTDOOR RECREATION

AMERICAN FORESTRY ASSOCIATION, 1319 18th St., NW, Washington, DC 20036.

ASSOCIATION OF INTERPRETIVE NATURALISTS, 6700 Needwood Road, Derwood, MD   20855.

NATIONAL PARKS AND CONSERVATION ASSOCIATION, 1701 18th St., NW, Washington, DC   20009.

NATIONAL RECREATION AND PARK ASSOCIATION, 1601 N. Kent St., Arlington, VA   22209.

NATIONAL WILDLIFE FEDERATION, 1412 16th St., NW, Washington, DC 20036.

NATIONAL SOCIETY FOR PARK RESOURCES, 1601 N. Kent St., Arlington, VA   22209.

SIERRA CLUB, 530 Bush St., San Francisco, CA   94108.

WESTERN INTERPRETERS ASSOCIATION, 6986 La Jolla Blvd., La Jolla, CA 92037.

WILDERNESS SOCIETY, 1901 Pennsylvania Ave., NW, Washington, DC 20006.

FORESTRY

AMERICAN FOREST INSTITUTE, 1619 Massachusetts Ave., NW, Washington, DC   20036.

AMERICAN FORESTRY ASSOCIATION, 1319 18th St., NW, Washington, DC 20036.

AMERICAN PAPER INSTITUTE, INC., 260 Madison Ave., New York, NY 10016.

AMERICAN PULPWOOD ASSOCIATION, 1619 Massachusetts Ave., NW, Washington, DC   20036.

FOREST FARMERS ASSOCIATION, 4 Executive Park East, NE, Atlanta, GA 30329.

NATIONAL FOREST PRODUCTS ASSOCIATION, 1619 Massachusetts Ave., NW, Washington, DC   20036.

SOCIETY OF AMERICAN FORESTERS, 5400 Grosvenor Lane, Washington, DC   20014.

WESTERN FORESTRY AND CONSERVATION ASSOCIATION, 1326 American Bank Bldg., Portland, OR   97205.

FRESHWATER RESOURCE MANAGEMENT

AMERICAN FISHERIES SOCIETY, 5410 Grosvenor Lane, Bethesda, MD 20014.

AMERICAN INSTITUTE OF BIOLOGICAL SCIENCES, 1401 Wilson Blvd., Arlington, VA   22209.

AMERICAN INSTITUTE OF FISHERY RESEARCH BIOLOGISTS, 1226 Skyline Drive, Edmonds, WA   98020.

AMERICAN SOCIETY OF ICHTHYOLOGISTS AND HERPETOLOGISTS, c/o National Marine Fisheries Services, Systematics Laboratory, U.S. National Museum, Washington, DC   20560.

BASS RESEARCH FOUNDATION, P. O. Box 99, Starkville, MS   39759.

INTERNATIONAL ASSOCIATION OF FISH AND WILDLIFE AGENCIES, 1412 16th St., NW, Washington, DC   20036.

SPORT FISHING INSTITUTE, Suite 801, 608 13th St., NW, Washington, DC 20005.

WILDLIFE BIOLOGY AND MANAGEMENT

AMERICAN ASSOCIATION OF ZOOLOGICAL PARKS AND AQUARIUMS, Oglebay Park, Wheeling, WV   26003.

AMERICAN COMMITTEE FOR INTERNATIONAL CONSERVATION, INC., Suite 611, 7101 Wisconsin Ave., NW, Washington, DC   20014.

AMERICAN FISHERIES SOCIETY, 5410 Grosvenor Lane, Bethesda, MD 20014.

AMERICAN FORESTRY ASSOCIATION, THE, 1319 18th St., NW, Washington, DC   20036.

AMERICAN HUMANE ASSOCIATION, THE, Box 1266, Denver, CO   80201.

AMERICAN ORNITHOLOGISTS' UNION, INC., National Museum of Natural History, Smithsonian Institution, Washington, DC   20560.

AMERICAN SOCIETY OF MAMMALOGISTS, SECTION OF MAMMALS, CARNEGIE MUSEUM OF NATURAL HISTORY, 4400 Forbes Ave., Pittsburgh, PA 15213.

CONSERVATION FOUNDATION, THE, 1717 Massachusetts Ave., NW, Washington, DC   20036.

DEFENDERS OF WILDLIFE, 1244 19th St., NW, Washington, DC   20036.

DUCKS UNLIMITED, INC., P.O. Box 66330, Chicago, IL   60666.

ENVIRONMENTAL DEFENSE FUND, INC., 527 Madison Ave., New York, NY   10022.

ENVIRONMENTAL POLICY CENTER, 317 Pennsylvania Ave., SE, Washington, DC   20003.

HUMANE SOCIETY OF THE UNITED STATES, THE, 2100 L St., NW, Washington, DC   20037.

INTERNATIONAL ASSOCIATION OF FISH AND WILDLIFE AGENCIES, 1412 16th St., NW, Washington, DC   20036.

IZAAK WALTON LEAGUE OF AMERICA, INC., THE, 1800 North Kent St., Suite 806, Arlington, VA   22209.

NATIONAL AUDUBON SOCIETY, 950 Third Ave., New York, NY   10022.

NATIONAL PARKS AND CONSERVATION ASSOCIATION, 1701 18th St., NW, Washington, DC   20009.

NATIONAL WILD TURKEY FEDERATION INC., THE, Wild Turkey Building, P.O. Box 467, Edgefield, SC   29824.

NATIONAL WILDLIFE FEDERATION, 1412 16th St., NW, Washington, DC 20036.

NATIONAL WILDLIFE REFUGE ASSOCIATION, P.O. Box 124, Winona, MN 55987.

NATURAL RESOURCES COUNCIL OF AMERICA, P.O. Box 20, Tracys Landing, MD   20869.

NATURE CONSERVANCY, THE, Suite 800, 1800 N. Kent St., Arlington, VA 22209.

NEW YORK ZOOLOGICAL SOCIETY, The Zoological Park, Bronx, NY 10460.

NORTH AMERICAN WOLF SOCIETY, P.O. Box 118, Eatonville, WA 98328.

RACHEL CARSON TRUST FOR THE LIVING ENVIRONMENT, INC., 8940 Jones Mill Road, Washington, DC   20015.

RENEWABLE NATURAL RESOURCES FOUNDATION, 5400 Grosvenor Lane, Bethesda, MD   20014.

RUFFED GROUSE SOCIETY OF NORTH AMERICA, 555 E. Main St., Kingwood, WV   26537.

SIERRA CLUB, 530 Bush St., San Francisco, CA   94108.

SOCIETY FOR RANGE MANAGEMENT, 2120 S. Birch St., Denver, CO 80222.

SOCIETY OF AMERICAN FORESTERS, 5400 Grosvenor Lane, Washington, DC   20014.

WHOOPING CRANE CONSERVATION ASSOCIATION, INC., 3000 Meadowlark Dr., Sierra Vista, AR   85635.

WILDLIFE DISEASE ASSOCIATION, P.O. Box 886, Ames, IA   60010.

WILDLIFE MANAGEMENT INSTITUTE, 1000 Vermont Ave., NW, 709 Wire Building, Washington, DC   20005.

WILDLIFE SOCIETY, THE, Suite 611, 7101 Wisconsin Ave., NW, Washington, DC   20014.

WORLD WILDLIFE FUND, 1601 Connecticut Ave., Washington, DC 20009.

MARINE AND ESTUARINE RESOURCE MANAGEMENT

AMERICAN FISHERIES SOCIETY, 5410 Grosvenor Lane, Bethesda, MD 20014.

AMERICAN INSTITUTE OF FISHERY RESEARCH BIOLOGISTS, 1226 Skyline Drive, Edmonds, WA   98020.

AMERICAN SOCIETY OF ICHTHYOLOGISTS AND HERPETOLOGISTS, c/o U.S. National Museum, Washington, DC   20560.

AMERICAN SOCIETY OF LIMNOLOGY AND OCEANOGRAPHY, DEPARTMENT OF ZOOLOGY NJ-15, UNIVERSITY OF WASHINGTON, Seattle, WA   98195.

ESTUARINE RESEARCH SOCIETY, ENVIRONMENTAL PROTECTION AGENCY, ANNAPOLIS FIELD OFFICE, ANNAPOLIS SCIENCE CENTER, Annapolis, MD 21403.

COASTAL SOCIETY, P. O. Box 34405, Bethesda, MD   20034.

NATIONAL COALITION FOR MARINE CONSERVATION, P. O. Box 23298, Savannah, GA   31403.

NATIONAL MARINE EDUCATION ASSOCIATION, 546 Presidio Blvd., San Francisco, CA   94129.

NATIONAL OCEANOGRAPHIC ASSOCIATION, 200 L St., NW, Washington, DC   20036.

SPORT FISHING INSTITUTE, Suite 801, 608 13th St., NW, Washington, DC 20005.

WORLD MARICULTURE SOCIETY, DEPARTMENT OF FISHERIES, LOUISIANA STATE UNIVERSITY, Baton Rouge, LA   70808.

NATIONAL SHELLFISHERIES ASSOCIATION, c/o NATIONAL MARINE FISHERIES SERVICE, Milford, CT   06460.

RANGE MANAGEMENT

SOCIETY FOR RANGE MANAGEMENT, 2760 West Fifth Ave., Denver, CO 80204.

SOCIETY OF AMERICAN FORESTERS, 5400 Grosvenor Lane, Washington, DC   20014.

SOIL CONSERVATION SOCIETY OF AMERICA, 7515 NE Ankeny Road, Ankeny, IA   50021.

WATERSHED MANAGEMENT

Society of American Foresters, 5400 Grosvenor Lane, Washington, DC   20014.

The American Forestry Association, 1319 18th St., NW, Washington, DC   20036.

American Water Resources Association. St. Anthony Falls Hydraulic Laboratory, Minneapolis, MN   55414.

American Geophysical Union, Hydrology Section, 1909 K St., NW, Washington, DC   20006.

Water Resources Association of the Delaware River Basin, 901 Stephen Girard Building, 21 So. 12th St., Philadelphia, PA 19107.

U.S. Water Resources Council, 2120 L St., NW, Washington, DC 20037.

Soil Conservation Society of America, 7515 Ankeny Road, Ankeny, IA   50021.

National Watershed Congress, 1025 Vermont Ave., NW, Washington, DC   20005.

Association of University Watershed Scientists, Department of Earth Resources, Colorado State University, Fort Collins, CO 80523.

BIOLOGY

Scientific and technical organizations concerned with biology in its relation to the conservation and management of renewable natural resources.

American Institute of Biological Sciences, 1401 Wilson Boulevard, Arlington, VA   22209.

American Society of Mammalogists, c/o Section of Mammals, Carnegie Museum of Natural History, 4400 Forbes Ave., Pittsburgh, PA   15213.

American Society of Microbiology, 1913 I St. NW, Washington, DC 20006.

American Society of Naturalists, c/o Botany, Genetics, and Development, Cornell University, Ithaca, NY   14853.

AMERICAN SOCIETY OF ZOOLOGISTS, Box 2739 CALIFORNIA LUTHERAN COLLEGE, Thousand Oaks, CA   91360.

BOTANICAL SOCIETY OF AMERICA, c/o DEPARTMENT OF BOTANY, UNIVERSITY OF TEXAS, Austin, TX   78703.

ENTOMOLOGICAL SOCIETY OF AMERICA, 4603 Calvert Road, College Park, MD   20740.

ECOLOGICAL SOCIETY OF AMERICA, c/o DEPARTMENT OF NATURAL AND ECONOMICAL RESOURCES, 116 West Jones Street, Raleigh, NC   27607.

LAND USE

Many organizations are concerned with land use, especially in its relation to natural resource conservation and management. Indeed, most of the organizations listed in the preceding sections of this appendix are involved in land use as it affects one or more particular resources.

In addition to the individual resource organizations named, the following have policies oriented to land use.

COUNCIL OF STATE GOVERNMENTS, 444 North Capitol St., Washington, DC   20001.

LEAGUE OF WOMEN VOTERS OF THE U.S., 1730 M St., NW, Washington, DC   20036.

NATIONAL ASSOCIATION OF COUNTIES, 1735 New York Ave., NW, Washington, DC   20006.

URBAN LAND INSTITUTE, 1200 18th St., NW, Washington, DC   20036.

Index

DISCARD

BETHANY

DISCARD.